AF602132

The

Art of Being Alone

Lydia Sterling

ISBN: 978-1-945-303-48-7 Paperback

ISBN: 978-1-945-303-50-0 Ebook

ISBN: 978-1-945-303-51-7 Hardcover

The Art of Being Alone

by Lydia Sterling

Description

Are you navigating a season of solitude, wondering if a truly fulfilling life is still possible when you're walking alone? Do you sometimes feel the weight of societal expectations, suggesting that being alone means being unfulfilled? Are you yearning to transform your current solitude from a place of uncertainty into a powerful path for personal growth and divine connection?

Perhaps you've faced divorce, profound loss, or simply haven't found your way yet, leaving you questioning God's plan for your life. If so, The Art of Being Alone is for you.

Lydia Sterling, with over two decades of experience as a writer, coach, and consultant, and a heart deeply rooted in Christ, understands these feelings intimately. She knows that while we are designed for connection, solitude is not an end, but a powerful new beginning. Through her own journey through profound heartbreak and a deep understanding of God's unfailing love, Lydia beautifully illustrates how life's solitary moments can lead to true happiness and a life of fullness. The Art of Being Alone is a heartfelt guide providing you with all the tools you need to embrace your alone season, deepen your faith, and discover the beautiful life God intends for you.

In this book, you will discover: - How to transform feelings of loss and heartbreak into opportunities for profound personal and spiritual renewal. - Practical strategies for reframing solitude from isolation into a sacred space for self-discovery and divine connection. - Powerful faith-based principles for building emotional resilience and healing from past events that led to aloneness. - A clear framework for building financial security and independence, aligning your resources with God's principles of stewardship. –

Techniques for creating meaningful connections and setting healthy boundaries to protect your solo strength. - Inspiring ways to identify your unique God-given calling and live out your purpose, even when walking alone. - Actionable steps to design fulfilling daily routines and cultivate inner peace while remaining open to future relationships. - And much more to empower your journey toward a joyful and prosperous solo life.

You might feel your unique circumstances make embracing solitude impossible, or perhaps you doubt you can truly find joy without a partner or family by your side. Lydia's empathetic guidance, rooted in both personal experience and divine wisdom, offers a compassionate path forward, showing you that God’s plan for a beautiful, fulfilling life is accessible to you, no matter your current situation.

If you are ready to transform your season of solitude into a vibrant, purposeful new beginning filled with God's love and prosperity, then grab The Art of Being Alone today and unlock the joyful life you were meant to live!

About the Author

Lydia Sterling is a compassionate guide dedicated to helping you discover a path to a happy, loving, and prosperous life, even when you find yourself walking alone. With a heart rooted in Christ, she beautifully illustrates how life's solitary moments can lead to true happiness and a life of fullness.

Drawing on over two decades as a writer, coach, and consultant, Lydia brings a wealth of experience and an MBA education to her work. However, it was her deep understanding that many circumstances can lead to being alone, whether through divorce, loss, or simply not yet finding your way—that profoundly shaped her mission to help others.

Lydia believes that while we are designed for connection, being alone is not an end, but a new beginning. She passionately shares that you can still live a wonderful, fulfilling, and beautiful life that God intends for you to have. Her message empowers you to embrace this chapter, knowing that God has a perfect plan for your life, no matter your current situation.

In her book, The Art of Being Alone, Lydia offers heartfelt encouragement and guidance to navigate times of stress and uncertainty. Her warm, personal approach resonates deeply, inspiring you to transform your understanding of solitude. Join Lydia on a journey to unlock the joy and purpose that God intends for your life, ensuring that your path, no matter how solitary it may seem, is filled with love and prosperity.

Table of Contents

Introduction

It seems almost blasphemous to suggest that being alone might be a gift, a sacred pause in the symphony of life, especially in a world that constantly broadcasts the merits of connection and partnership. We are bombarded with images of togetherness, sold on the idea that our happiness and worth are inextricably tied to another person.

This cultural narrative often casts solitude as a temporary state to be endured, a void to be filled, rather than a fertile ground for profound growth and divine communion.

Yet, beneath the surface of this relentless clamor, a quiet, undeniable truth persists some of the most transformative moments, the deepest revelations, and the most robust periods of self-discovery emerge not from crowded rooms or bustling relationships, but from the stillness of a solitary heart.

This book dares to challenge that prevailing dogma, proposing a counter-narrative: that your season of aloneness is not an unfortunate detour, but a divinely orchestrated pathway to a life far richer, more purposeful, and more deeply connected to the source of all love than you might currently imagine.

It invites you to reconsider what you think you know about solitude, urging you to see it not as a curse to overcome, but as an invitation to embrace, a powerful opportunity to build a life so vibrant and full that it redefines the very meaning of happiness. Here, you will discover that being alone is not an end, but a new beginning, a unique chapter where God is waiting to reveal His magnificent plan for you.

Perhaps you've felt the sting of a well meaning relative's question about your relationship status, the quiet ache of scrolling through picture-perfect couples on social media, or the subtle but pervasive sense that something is missing from your life because you're not partnered. You might be navigating the aftermath of a profound loss—a marriage ended by divorce, a cherished spouse called home to God, or perhaps you're young, still searching for your path, wondering why connection feels so elusive.

The pressure to conform, to find "the one," often leaves you feeling inadequate or overlooked, struggling with feelings of loneliness even when surrounded by others. Beneath these surface anxieties, however, lies a deeper yearning: a desire not just to fill a void, but to experience genuine contentment, to live a life brimming with purpose and love, to feel whole and complete irrespective of your relational status.

You crave an existence where your happiness isn't contingent on external circumstances, where you feel truly seen and valued, and where you can step into each new day with confidence and an unwavering sense of divine direction. This yearning, this desire for a truly meaningful and joyful life, is not a frivolous wish; it is a spiritual whisper, guiding you toward a profound truth about your own inherent worth and the boundless love God has for you, right here, right now.

Imagine shedding the weight of societal expectations, no longer measuring your worth by your relationship status or allowing the past to dictate your present joy. Picture a life where solitude isn't a burden but a launchpad, propelling you into unprecedented seasons of personal growth, spiritual intimacy, and vibrant purpose.

This book is your compassionate guide to precisely that transformation, moving you from the quiet corners of perceived loneliness into the expansive landscape of a truly abundant existence. You will journey from feeling defined by what you lack to being empowered by what you possess: a profound connection with your Creator, an unshakeable inner peace, and a clear vision for your future.

We will explore how to cultivate Faithful Independence, building a foundation of self-reliance rooted in divine trust that enables you to navigate any challenge with grace and an unyielding spirit. You'll learn to embrace what I call New Beginnings Alone, recognizing these moments not as closures, but as powerful openings for God to unfold His most beautiful designs, orchestrating pathways you never knew existed.

This isn't about merely enduring solitude; it's about actively creating a Thriving Solo Life—one filled with passion, meaningful contributions, and genuine delight, irrespective of whether a partner stands by your side. Prepare to discover the joy of Prosperous Singlehood, where prosperity extends beyond financial abundance to encompass spiritual richness, emotional resilience, deep self-awareness, and an overflowing sense of purpose.

You will wake each morning with a profound sense of peace, knowing that every step you take is guided by a loving hand, moving you closer to the person God created you to be. This is a promise of profound renewal, where you will not only survive being alone but truly flourish, understanding that God's Alone Plan is meticulously crafted for your ultimate happiness and fulfillment, illuminating a path where every solitary moment becomes a sacred opportunity for divine encounter and personal triumph.

My own journey through unexpected turns and profound losses has led me to this understanding, not as an academic theory, but as a lived truth.

Like many of you, I have walked through seasons of deep solitude born from circumstances I never anticipated—the sharp pain of divorce, the indescribable heartache of losing a child. These were moments that could have shattered my spirit, leaving me adrift and defined by what was lost.

Instead, through a steadfast reliance on Christ, they became crucibles for growth, forging a compassion and resilience that now fuel my mission. With over two decades as a writer, coach, and consultant, and an MBA education providing a robust framework for practical solutions, my professional life has equipped me to distill complex ideas into actionable insights. However, it is my heart, rooted in the unwavering belief that God has a perfect plan for every life, that truly guides my approach. I've learned firsthand that even in our deepest solitude, God is intimately present, weaving a tapestry of purpose from threads of pain.

This isn't just a book I've researched; it's a life I've lived, a testament to the truth that being alone is not an end, but a new beginning, an opportunity to cultivate a wonderfully fulfilling and beautiful existence precisely as God intends. My commitment is to share the wisdom gained from these experiences, helping you discover the same profound joy and purpose that can emerge from your own solitary path.

Throughout these pages, you will acquire more than just insight; you will gain a comprehensive toolkit for transforming your solo journey into an unparalleled adventure of self-discovery and spiritual depth.

You will learn to reframe solitude from a perceived lack into a powerful catalyst for growth, understanding how societal myths about aloneness often obscure God's divine purpose for your season. This book will guide you in building a robust spiritual practice for your solo life, establishing daily routines rooted in intentional prayer, engaging with scripture, and incorporating contemplative practices that foster an unwavering connection with God.

Furthermore, you will uncover potent strategies for healing from the events that led to your aloneness, acknowledging your pain and loss, and leveraging faith as a powerful catalyst for emotional resilience and renewal, integrating insights from psychotherapy with spiritual wisdom. We will delve into practical steps for discovering and developing your authentic self, leveraging your alone time to explore passions, pursue continuous learning, and unleash your creative expression.

You'll also find actionable guidance on building financial security and independence, understanding biblical principles of stewardship to create a sustainable financial plan that supports your Thriving Solo Life and ensures Prosperous Singlehood. Most importantly, you will learn to create meaningful connections without losing yourself, setting healthy boundaries, identifying supportive communities, and engaging authentically while preserving your solo strength. You will emerge from this journey not only resilient but vibrant, equipped to embrace your unique God-given calling and to live a life overflowing with joy, purpose, and abundant love, irrespective of your relational status.

This journey within these pages is not one of mere survival, but of glorious revelation. It's an invitation to see your life through a new lens—a divine lens that illuminates the profound beauty and purpose woven into every solitary moment.

With a compassionate heart and unwavering faith, I will walk alongside you, offering encouragement, practical tools, and a deep wellspring of hope. This is your opportunity to shed old narratives, embrace God's perfect design for your current season, and step boldly into a future brimming with joy, prosperity, and authentic love.

There is a magnificent life waiting for you, a vibrant existence carefully curated by the Creator, and it begins right here, right now, as you open your heart to The Art of Being Alone. Together, let us embark on this sacred path, unlocking the extraordinary possibilities that await when you truly discover the power and beauty of your New Beginnings Alone and commit to living a Thriving Solo Life as God intended.

Chapter 1

My Journey Through Loss and Solitude

Facing the Darkness of Divorce

Divorce dismantles the mental architecture meticulously built over years—the assumptions about who you'd grow old with, whose voice you'd hear at breakfast, what holidays would look like when your children had children.

One moment, you're planning a vacation together; the next, you're dividing furniture and learning to sleep in a bed that feels cavernous and wrong. Emotional fallout rarely follows neat stages. Anger erupts at 3 a.m. when a specific lie resurfaces.

Confusion settles in when you instinctively reach for your phone to text the person you're now legally separating from. Grief manifests not as a single wave but as dozens of small deaths—the end of shared jokes, mutual friends who awkwardly choose sides, the particular way someone made coffee that you'll never taste again.

The inherent ambiguity of divorce creates profound disorientation. Death, for instance, offers finality and communal rituals of mourning; divorce does not. Instead, it leaves you navigating a strange twilight where the person still exists, sometimes in the same town, occasionally in your text messages about logistics. You are expected to function normally, show up to work, parent effectively, make rational decisions—while internally, everything feels like static.

Suppressing these emotions only compounds the damage. Meaningful healing begins by acknowledging that what you're feeling, however chaotic or contradictory, deserves space and attention. Then write down why you are so angry. No wait you are not angry you are downright mad. Yes, mad. Write it down 100 times 1000 times. Then tear up the paper. It works. This is not weakness; this is the necessary first step toward a new beginning that God has already prepared for you.

Divorce doesn't just end a marriage, it thrusts you into a space where isolation and solitude collide, and knowing the difference between them can reshape your entire healing journey.

Isolation traps you in cycles of pain. It keeps you replaying arguments, scrolling through old photos, torturing yourself with endless "what if" scenarios that lead nowhere. But solitude? Solitude is different. It's a sacred space where you can rebuild from the inside out, free from distractions and the noise of expectations. Here, in the quiet, you discover who you are beyond the marriage that ended.

Three practices anchored me when everything felt adrift: journaling transformed my tangled emotions into words I could finally see and understand. Writing "I feel abandoned" on paper somehow made the pain less consuming, giving it shapes and limits. Prayer became my lifeline—not just words cast into the void, but genuine conversation with God, seeking His comfort when my own thoughts spiraled. And community support, whether through a recovery group or trusted friends, reminded me I wasn't alone in this devastation.

Isaiah 41:10 (KJV): "Fear thou not; for I am with thee: be not dismayed; for I am thy God: I will strengthen thee; yea, I will help thee; yea, I will uphold thee with the right hand of my righteousness."

These aren't magic solutions that erase grief overnight. They're anchors that hold you steady while the storm passes, transforming your darkest moments into doorways toward healing.

Months after my divorce, I sat in a coffee shop watching couples laugh together, and the ache nearly sent me home. But I stayed.

That small act of defiance—choosing to exist in the world despite the pain—marked the beginning of something I couldn't yet name. Renewal doesn't arrive with fanfare. It creeps in through tiny moments: the morning you wake up without that crushing weight on your chest, the afternoon you laugh genuinely for the first time in weeks, the evening you realize you've gone hours without thinking about what you lost. These fragments don't erase the devastation. They simply prove that devastation isn't permanent.

One Wednesday, a stranger at church asked how I was doing, and instead of the rehearsed "I'm fine," I told the truth. She didn't offer platitudes or try to fix me. She just listened, then shared her own story of loss and unexpected grace. That conversation became a turning point—not because it solved anything, but because it reminded me that God works through broken people reaching toward other broken people.

Your path won't mirror mine. But the principle holds: divine intervention often looks like ordinary moments infused with extraordinary meaning, quietly revealing new directions when the old ones disappear.

The Heartbreak of Losing a Child

Losing a child inverts the natural order of existence in ways that defy language.

Parents aren't supposed to bury their children. That fundamental violation creates a grief so disorienting that even basic tasks—showering, answering the phone, choosing what to eat—become monumental. This grief doesn't follow stages or timelines. You might feel numb for weeks, then collapse in the cereal aisle because your daughter loved that brand.

Anger erupts at parents complaining about college tuition, a milestone you'll never reach. Guilt arrives in waves: the appointment you almost rescheduled, the argument the week before, the irrational conviction that you should have known, should have prevented, should have traded places. Some mornings you wake up believing it was a nightmare, those seconds before reality crashes back feeling almost crueler than the loss itself.

Well-meaning people offer phrases that sting rather than comfort: "They're in a better place" when you'd give anything for them to be here. "God needed another angel" when you needed your child. These words, however kindly intended, reveal how desperately uncomfortable others feel with grief this profound.

Acknowledging these feelings—the rage, the bargaining with God, the moments you forget they're gone—isn't weakness. It's the only honest response to catastrophic loss. Suppressing them creates pressure that eventually erupts in destructive ways: addiction, isolation, relationships fractured by unspoken pain. Healing begins not with moving past these emotions but with allowing them room to exist, giving yourself permission to grieve without apologizing for the depth of your sorrow.

Psalm 34:18 (KJV): "The Lord is nigh unto them that are of a broken heart; and seventh such as be of a contrite spirit."

When Sarah's seven-year-old son died from complications during routine surgery, her first response wasn't grief—it was fury at God. For three weeks, she refused to pray, rejected visits from her pastor, and told friends who suggested divine comfort to leave her house. She described those weeks as standing in a dark room, screaming at someone she wasn't sure existed anymore.

Then something unexpected happened. She found herself driving to the cemetery at dawn, sitting on the grass, and speaking aloud, prayers exactly, but raw accusations mixed with memories of her son's laugh. That honest conversation, absent any theological politeness, became the thread pulling her back toward faith.

Doubt doesn't disqualify you from relationship with God. The biblical figure Job lost his children and spent chapters hurling questions at heaven, demanding answers that never came in the form he wanted. What arrived instead was presence—not explanation, but companionship through incomprehensible pain. Wrestling with God requires believing He's substantial enough to withstand your anger.

Sarah eventually returned to church, but her faith looked different—less about certainty, more about showing up in the dark. She stopped expecting answers and started recognizing sustenance: strength she didn't manufacture herself, moments of unexpected peace that felt like grace was arriving unannounced. This transformed understanding became her pathway to deeper spiritual growth, proving that questioning can lead us closer to God's heart than pretending ever could.

Sarah's transformation didn't happen in isolation. Two months after her son's death, a friend texted her the number of a woman named Claire whose daughter had died three years earlier.

When Sarah finally called, Claire didn't offer platitudes or false comfort. She said, "Tuesdays are still hard for me," and described buying her daughter's favorite cereal by accident, standing in the grocery aisle crying. That specificity—the admission that years later, grief still ambushed her—gave Sarah something precious: permission to not be fixed. The acknowledgment that healing doesn't mean forgetting, that some wounds transform but never fully close.

Finding others who've endured child loss creates something clinical support can't replicate. These people don't flinch when you mention your child's name. They don't change the subject or rush to comfort. A support group, whether formal organizations like The Compassionate Friends or intimate gatherings, becomes sacred ground where your deepest pain doesn't make others uncomfortable.

Yet community fails when it becomes performance. Healthy support acknowledges different grief without ranking it. It allows silence. It tolerates anger at God, envy toward parents with living children, and those bewildering moments when you laugh at something stupid and feel guilty immediately after.

Connection doesn't erase pain; it distributes the weight so you're not carrying it alone every hour.

Channeling grief begins with micro-commitments, not grand declarations. Beverly Chappell, after losing her son Doug to cystic fibrosis in 1981, initially responded to his friends' grief by simply opening her home to them. She listened, offered a safe space, and allowed them to share their pain. It wasn't about formal therapy; it was about showing up and bearing witness. That small gesture became structure when structure felt impossible.

Within a year, this informal support evolved into The Dougy Center for Grieving Children & Families, established in Portland, Oregon, in 1982. No formal agenda. Just a place for coffee, tissues, and silence when needed. Chappell didn't position herself as healed or expert—she showed up grieving, unsure how to navigate holidays without her son.

Authenticity mattered more than advice. Grieving families found someone who wouldn't minimize their loss, or rush toward a closure that doesn't exist.

Purpose emerges from this repetition. Not because pain disappears, but because witnessing transforms it. Each person Chappell sat with—each raw story she absorbed without flinching—added weight to her son's absence, made his brief life ripple outward in ways she never anticipated. The loss remained devastating. But accompanying others through similar devastation gave her mornings a reason beyond surviving them.

Start where you are: one phone call, one written story shared, one hour volunteering with bereaved families. Let purpose grow incrementally, awkwardly, imperfectly.

Embracing Solitude as a Pathway to Growth

Tomorrow morning, give yourself fifteen minutes. Not for meditation or journaling—just sitting with yourself, phone turned off, no podcast filling the silence. Set a timer if you need the boundary but resist the urge to turn this into something productive.

Restlessness will arrive first, that familiar itch to check something, fix something, move. Let it come. Don't obey it.

When the discomfort peaks, a question often surfaces: What am I avoiding by staying so busy?

Don't force an answer. The question itself begins with the work of transformation.

Create a solitude ritual that anchors your week—something beyond typical self-care, something that feels real. Some people visit a quiet cemetery weekly, sitting on a bench to reflect in the stillness. Others walk the same trail at dawn, using the rhythm of their steps to process unspoken thoughts. The location matters less than the consistency. Your body learns that this time belongs to truth, not performance. This is where God speaks clearest—not in the noise, but in the sacred quiet you create for Him.

Try this: spend one full day without explaining yourself to anyone. No justifying your choices, defending your feelings, or managing perceptions. Notice how often you preemptively narrate your decisions, translating your interior life for external consumption. The silence teaches you how much energy you've been spending on performance instead of presence.

Keep a record of what you discover. Write down the thought that arrived during your silent fifteen minutes, the decision that clarified on the Thursday bench, the anger you finally felt without an audience. These fragments accumulate into something precious: evidence of your actual life, the one hidden beneath all the explaining.

Solitude isn't preparation for being better for others.

It's remembering who you are when no one's watching—and discovering that God has been there all along.

Solitude, when embraced with intention, becomes a crucible for transformation. The quiet work of learning to sit still, to resist the clamor of external noise, forms a foundation that endures far beyond any season of aloneness. This inner strength doesn't vanish when relationships return or circumstances shift—it becomes the bedrock upon which you engage with everything and everyone that follows.

Consider what this sacred time has already cultivated within you.

Genuine self-sufficiency emerges not from isolation, but from discovering you can exist fully in your own company. Those fifteen minutes of morning silence taught you something profound: inner peace doesn't require constant external validation. You learned to be present with yourself, to find strength without collapsing into distraction or needing an audience for your thoughts. This is faithful independence at its truest—a life no longer driven by the exhausting cycle of seeking approval.

The grace of this journey lies in what comes next. You don't abandon these hard-won insights when new chapters unfold. Instead, you carry them forward—into relationships that honor your wholeness, into purpose that flows from genuine calling, into the demanding work of loving others without losing yourself. The strength forged in solitude enables you to love without desperation, contribute without needing applause, and stand resilient when loss inevitably arrives again.

Some mornings will still feel hollow. Some days will challenge everything you've built.

But you'll return to that familiar place—whether it's a quiet room, a walking trail, or simply the stillness within—and remember here, you encountered yourself without pretense. Here, God met you in the silence and confirmed that being alone was never abandonment, but divine opportunity. This is your foundation now, the ground beneath every step forward into life awaiting you.

Chapter 2

Challenging the Myth That Alone Equals Unfulfilled

Identifying Societal Pressures Surrounding Solitude

Marriage rates in the United States peaked in 1972 before beginning a steady descent, and by the mid-2000s, more adults lived alone than ever before in recorded history. Politicians blamed individualism. Preachers warned of moral decay. Magazine covers declared a loneliness epidemic.

Yet this modern view of solitude as a problem contradicts centuries of human experience. Throughout history, solitude often held a revered status. Desert fathers withdrew into caves seeking divine encounters, and mystics isolated themselves by calling, not weakness. Philosophers from Seneca to Montaigne championed withdrawal as essential to clarity. The Roman concept of otium—reflection leisure apart from social demands—was considered the highest use of time.

Silence carried status; being alone signaled strength and discipline.

Medieval anchorites voluntarily walled themselves into cells attached to churches, honored by communities as spiritually advanced, not damaged. The shift arrived with industrialization. Factories required synchronized bodies. Capitalism commodified togetherness with products marketed to couples and families. Freud reframed solitude as symptoms, not choice. Suburban planning eliminated space for withdrawal, and by the mid-twentieth century, solitude transformed from spiritual practice to social failure.

This redefinition didn't originate in theology or wisdom, but in economic systems profiting from our fear of being alone.

Media functions as society's most powerful storytelling engine, and for decades, it has broadcast one relentless message: solitude signals something broken. Television sitcoms revolve around groups of dynamic friends gathered in coffee shops, families navigating chaos together, coworkers forming makeshift tribes. Characters who prefer solitude are coded as damaged, antisocial, or desperately waiting for rescue.

Romantic comedies structure themselves around a foundational lie: that completeness arrives only through coupling.

The protagonist's journey ends not with self-discovery but with another person filling a presumed void. Solo moments exist only as temporary states before the real story begins. Advertising amplifies this distortion further—insurance companies sell policies with images of multigenerational gatherings, cruise lines show couples watching sunsets, food brands position their products at crowded tables. Even pharmaceutical ads depict the "after" state as social reintegration, as though standing alone becomes the symptom requiring treatment.

Social media algorithms prioritize content showing connection, celebration, togetherness. Posts depicting solitary activities receive fewer likes, lower engagement, reduced visibility. The message calcifies through repetition: being with others equals success; being alone equals something requiring correction. This isn't accidental. Markets require consumers who feel incomplete, who believe products and relationships will fill manufactured deficiencies.

Popular culture doesn't reflect reality—it constructs it, frame by frame, until we internalize scripts written by people profiting from our self-doubt.

Internalizing these cultural scripts exacts measurable psychological damage. Research extensively published by the American Psychological Association documents elevated cortisol levels—the stress hormone—in individuals experiencing prolonged social isolation. But here's what researchers discovered that should change how you view your alone time: similar spikes appear in people who feel socially inadequate despite frequent contact. Anxiety stems not from actual solitude but from perceived failure to meet societal benchmarks.

You carry this double burden: the practical reality of being alone and the shame of believing you shouldn't be.

Extensive clinical studies reveal that chronic loneliness increases inflammation markers comparable to cigarette smoking, elevates blood pressure, and disrupts sleep architecture. Yet the most insidious damage operates cognitively. Prolonged exposure to messaging that frames aloneness as pathological rewires your interpretation of neutral experiences. A quiet evening becomes evidence of inadequacy rather than rest. Eating alone shifts from practical necessity to public admission of social failure. Declining invitations—even when genuinely preferring solitude—triggers guilty cycles that erode self-trust.

Mental health professionals increasingly distinguish between loneliness and solitude, noting that the former involves distressing disconnection while the latter offers restorative privacy. The distinction collapses when culture refuses to recognize it. You begin monitoring your aloneness through others' eyes, performing busyness to avoid judgment, scheduling activities not from desire but from fear of appearing isolated.

Depression and anxiety don't emerge from solitude itself. They emerge from the relentless internal narrative that solitude means something is wrong with you—that your life, as currently structured, represents failure rather than a valid chapter in God's unfolding story for your purpose.

Reframing the Narrative: Alone Does Not Mean Unfulfilled

Cultural conditioning begins early, whispered into our consciousness before we even learn to question it. Count the children at the birthday party—a four-year-old's value suddenly measured in RSVPs. Watch the school cafeteria transform into a daily courtroom where eating alone delivers its own verdict: social failure. Listen as youth leaders insist that faith requires community, subtly teaching us that our private prayers somehow count less than worship offered in crowds.

These accumulated lessons calcify into belief.

When you sit alone at a restaurant, that familiar discomfort doesn't spring from the meal itself. It rises from internalized scripts playing on repeat: everyone here thinks something is wrong with me. The shame you feel. It wasn't born in your heart. It was taught, absorbed, conditioned into you by a culture terrified of stillness.

Religious communities can intensify this pressure, despite scripture celebrating wilderness encounters and Jesus himself withdrawing from crowds. Modern church culture emphasizes small groups, accountability partners, constant fellowship. Singles ministries frame singleness as a waiting period—a problem requiring pastoral intervention rather than a legitimate calling. The underlying message becomes unmistakable: spiritual maturity must look like visible connection.

The belief that alone equals unfulfilled didn't emerge from divine revelation. It emerged from systems—educational, religious, economic—that function more smoothly when individuals fear their own company. Recognizing this origin doesn't instantly eliminate your discomfort, but it does something powerful: it reveals that the voice condemning your solitude isn't God's voice at all.

Sarah Martinez spent thirteen years teaching fourth grade, then caring for her dying mother, then navigating a divorce that left her financially unstable and emotionally gutted. At forty-one, she found herself living alone for the first time in her adult life.

The first months brought predictable devastation, sleepless nights, weight loss, and a persistent sense of being unmade.

But something unexpected emerged around month seven. Sarah began using Sunday mornings differently. Instead of rushing to fill silence with television or frantic text conversations, she started walking the trail behind her apartment complex with nothing but a thermos of coffee. What she discovered wasn't peace, exactly. It was clarity. Walking alone, she finally heard thoughts she'd been drowning out for years: that she'd been performing her marriage rather than living it, that she'd confused being needed with being valued, that her identity had become dangerously tethered to others' approval. These weren't comfortable realizations, but they were true, and truth has a way of setting foundations for rebuilding.

Within eighteen months, Sarah had completed a certification program she'd postponed twice during her marriage, launched a tutoring practice that restored financial stability, and reconnected with painting—an abandoned passion from her twenties.

Her journal from that period doesn't describe triumph. It describes excavation: discovering preferences her ex-husband had dismissed, rebuilding decision-making muscles atrophied from years of compromise, learning that her thoughts held weight even when no one else heard them. Solitude didn't fix Sarah. It gave her uninterrupted space to remember who she'd been before loss, and to imagine who she might become after—a gift only silence could offer.

But reframing solitude isn't always straightforward and recognizing when it's failing you requires ruthless honesty. If Sarah had locked herself away for three years, refusing every invitation and avoiding all human contact, her solitude would have hardened into something dangerous. Withdrawal becomes pathological when it stops serving growth and starts protecting avoidance.

Pay attention to these warning signs: declining invitations not from genuine preference but from fear of judgment; obsessing over reconciliation fantasies instead of building your future; numbing emotional pain with substances, endless scrolling, or compulsive shopping rather than processing it. Healthy solitude brings discomfort that eventually yields insight—destructive isolation compounds discomfort into despair.

The exercises matter, but only if you have capacity for them.

Depression doesn't respond to inspirational nudges about finding yourself. Trauma doesn't dissolve because you bought beautiful journals. If getting out of bed requires heroic effort, if intrusive thoughts dominate your days, if you've lost dangerous weight or can't remember your last full night of sleep, these signals clinical distress requiring professional intervention. In such cases, well-meaning reframing exercises become demands on an already overdrawn account.

Sarah's journey worked because she paired solitude with accountability, attending a divorce recovery group monthly, maintaining contact with two trusted friends. Not constantly, but consistently. She let others spot when isolation was serving healing versus enabling hiding.

Reframing isn't about convincing yourself that aloneness feels wonderful. It's distinguishing between the pain of your circumstances, and the shame culture adds to that pain, then methodically dismantling the shame while honoring your grief.

Divine solitude isn't passive waiting—it's active cultivation of sacred space where God's voice rises above the noise. When you embrace aloneness as intentional rather than accidental, everything shifts.

Begin with fifteen uninterrupted minutes each morning before the world makes demands. Not productivity time—presence time. Brew coffee slowly. Sit without agenda. Notice what surfaces when distraction isn't an option. Your mind will scream urgent tasks to escape the discomfort. Let them pass like clouds across the sky. This is where divine whispers live—in the space between your anxious thoughts and the quiet you're brave enough to enter.

Create one weekly ritual that requires nothing from you. Sunday afternoon walks without destination. Saturday mornings at a café with a book you're not obligated to finish. The structure matters less than the consistency—your soul needs to learn that gentle, predictable solitude signals safety, not crisis. God meets us in rhythms, not chaos.

Journal three moments each week where you felt divine presence. Not grand revelations—sunlight through your kitchen window, unexpected kindness, relief after tears. Train your attention toward what's already there.

When shame whispers that you're eating dinner alone again, name it out loud. Spoken, it becomes manageable rather than suffocating.

This is your sacred space. Guard it fiercely.

Embracing Solitude as a Path to Self-Discovery

Choose one actual place where you won't be interrupted. Not someday, somewhere perfect—a real corner of your bedroom, a specific park bench, your car in that empty lot near the grocery store. Commit to fifteen minutes there, twice this week.

Bring nothing productive. No self-help books, no problem-solving podcasts, no phone angled for inspiration. Bring only a notebook and pen.

Write three sentences completing this prompt: "When no one is watching, I..." Don't filter for nobility. If the honest answer is "scroll until my eyes burn" or "replay arguments I'll never have," write it down. Solitude begins with truth, not performance.

Next, establish one weekly ritual requiring zero justification. Saturday morning coffee on the back steps. Wednesday evening walk with no destination. Sunday afternoon reading that serves no professional purpose. The point isn't the activity—it teaches your spirit that existing without productivity or witness holds profound value.

Isolation whispers you're hiding; solitude asks what you're discovering. If your alone time consistently numbs rather than clarifies, if it feeds fear instead of curiosity, that's valuable information. Adjust accordingly. Call the friend. Schedule the therapist. Solitude isn't suffering—it's sacred space for encountering both yourself and God.

Most people abandon their first solitude practice within the critical initial weeks. Not because solitude fails them—because discomfort arrives exactly when promised, and we misread the sensation as evidence we're doing something wrong.

Your mind will race during those first fifteen minutes. Thoughts will ricochet between grocery lists and decade-old humiliations. That's not failure. That's the noise you've been outrunning finally catching up, demanding to be heard. Your job isn't silencing it—it's staying present while it plays out, trusting that God is working even in the chaos of your wandering thoughts.

Lower the bar dramatically.

If you managed eight minutes before grabbing your phone, that's eight minutes of reclaimed territory. If your weekly ritual happened once this month instead of four times, you still created sacred space that didn't exist before. Progress compounds through repetition, not perfection. The Divine doesn't measure your devotion by flawless execution but by your willingness to return.

When you miss a week—and you will—return without apology or self-flagellation. The practice doesn't demand penance; it requires presence. Shame about inconsistency becomes another distraction, another way to avoid the actual work of showing up to meet God in the quiet.

Some discoveries feel exhilarating. Others land like stones in your chest—realizations about postponed dreams, compromised values, years spent performing someone else's script. Don't force gratitude for painful clarity. Acknowledgment precedes transformation. Write it down. Let it exist without immediately fixing it. God meets you in the messy middle, not the polished endpoint.

The worthiness of your solitude doesn't depend on profound insights or spiritual breakthroughs. It depends on your willingness to occupy unscheduled time without apologizing for existing. Start again tomorrow. Small, imperfect, repeated—that's how aloneness becomes discovery rather than exile.

In solitude's quiet hours, something profound shifts—you begin to hear God's voice more clearly than ever before. The chatter that once drowned out divine whispers' fades, replaced by a sacred stillness where spiritual truth becomes unmistakable. This isn't about seeking isolation from God; it's about discovering that He's been waiting for you in the silence all along.

Prayer transforms when you're alone. Without distractions competing for your attention, conversations with God deepen from hurried requests to genuine communion. You notice His presence in the morning light streaming through your window, in the rhythm of your own breath, in the inexplicable peace that settles over your spirit. These moments aren't accidentally divine appointments orchestrated specifically for your growth.

Scripture comes alive differently in solitude. Verses you've read dozens of times suddenly speak directly to your circumstances, as if written precisely for this season of your life. God uses your aloneness to reveal truths about your identity, your calling, and his unwavering faithfulness that crowds and noise would have obscured.

This spiritual clarity doesn't arrive overnight. It emerges gradually through consistent time spent in God's presence, through journaling prayers that map your evolving relationship with Him, through worship that's unperformed and unobserved. You're not just discovering yourself, you're discovering whose you are, and that changes everything.

Chapter 3

Understanding God's Plan for Your Alone Season

The Divine Design of Solitude

Moses spent forty years in the Midian desert before the burning bush—forty years tending sheep, walking barren ridges, living in obscurity while his people suffered under Pharaoh's whips.

This extended solitude prepared him.

Scripture consistently shows isolation as a crucible for profound change. Moses, before confronting empires, spent decades alone shedding his identity as an entitled Egyptian prince, becoming receptive to divine instruction. Jesus, prior to His ministry, was led by the Spirit into the wilderness for forty days of fasting and temptation. Paul, before proclaiming a gospel that altered history's course, spent three years in Arabian solitude following his Damascus Road experience, dismantling everything he thought he knew.

Deuteronomy 31:6, 8 (KJV) - Courage and God's unfailing presence: "Be strong and of a good courage, fear not, nor be afraid of them: for the Lord thy God, he it is that doth go with thee; he will not fail thee, nor forsake thee... And the Lord, he it is that doth go before thee; he will be with thee, he will not fail thee, neither forsake thee: fear not, neither be dismayed."

Solitude functions as a divine filter, removing the distractions that obscure clarity. While groups affirm our current identity, isolation reveals our potential. Moses found the desert's silence essential for hearing God's voice. Jesus required the wilderness to refine His mission before facing disciples, crowds, and escalating demands.

Your period of isolation may feel like exile. But considering how God used solitude to prepare these men, such times represent intentional space for growth—transforming nascent faith into deeply rooted conviction, equipping you for your unique purpose.

Transformation requires disruption. The wilderness doesn't polish you gently—it strips away what no longer serves, revealing the unvarnished truth beneath accumulated layers of performance and expectation.

This process feels brutal because it is. Solitude excavates questions you've avoided: Who am I when no one's applauding? What do I believe when community isn't reinforcing it? What desires persist when I stop performing for an audience? These profound questions are the raw material of spiritual formation—the uncomfortable work that crowds allow us to postpone indefinitely.

Paul's three years in Arabia weren't vacation.

He spent them dismantling a lifetime of certainty—every sermon he'd preached, every Pharisaic conviction he'd defended, every assumption about righteousness and God's favor. That solitary reckoning produced the theology that reshaped Christianity. Without those isolated years, he would have remained Saul: educated, zealous, and fundamentally unchanged.

Your aloneness creates identical opportunity because it removes the distractions that prevent honest assessment. You can't hear God's whisper in a crowd. You can't confront buried pain while maintaining social performance. You can't discover your actual self while constantly presenting the version others expect.

Solitude serves as sacred interruption—God pressing pause on your scripted life, creating space for the deeper work genuine transformation demands.

Spiritual atrophy happens quietly. You can attend every service, join every Bible study, master theological vocabulary, and still miss the fundamental question: Do you actually know God, or do you know about Him?

Most people confuse the two their entire lives.

A Barna Group study found that when asked to define 'a personal relationship with Jesus Christ,' only 51% of practicing Christians could articulate a robust, biblically based understanding. They can recite doctrine. They recognize borrowed language from sermons and worship songs.

But isolated, outside reinforcing environments, their faith feels abstract—secondhand conviction rather than lived encounter. Solitude exposes this gap because it removes the scaffolding. Without worship teams manufacturing emotion, without charismatic teachers providing pre-packaged insights, without the energy of collective singing masking your uncertainty, you discover what remains.

For many, the answer is unsettling: not much.

This revelation offers a profound opportunity for genuine faith. You cannot build authentic spiritual strength on someone else's foundation. Borrowed conviction collapses under pressure. Encounters forged in solitude, where you wrestle with God directly rather than consuming others' interpretations, create bedrock that external circumstances cannot erode.

Moses spent forty years alone before the burning bush. That solitude didn't diminish his capacity for leadership—it prepared him for it, stripping away borrowed Egyptian identity until only essential truth remained.

Your alone season isn't isolating you from spiritual community. It's preparing you to engage it authentically.

Invitations to Growth and Reflection

When Joseph languished in Pharaoh's prison, the text says God "was with him." Not rescuing him—with him. Two full years passed between interpreting the cupbearer's dream and standing before Pharaoh. Seven hundred and thirty days of stone walls and iron bars, where the only curriculum was waiting.

This period demonstrates God's purposeful work in seasons of waiting. The prison years honed Joseph from an arrogant boy who flaunted his dreams into a leader capable of saving nations. Potiphar's household taught administration. The false accusation taught integrity under injustice. The forgotten years after helping the cupbearer taught humility. Without each layer, Joseph would have become prime minister at seventeen—brilliant, gifted, and catastrophically unprepared for the weight of power.

Your solitude mirrors this intentional preparation. Though it may feel like exile, it often serves as sacred groundwork—not because God orchestrates your pain, but because He refuses to waste it. The 2 a.m. question, "Why am I still alone?" often has a profound answer: the person you are becoming requires conditions crowds cannot provide.

Without constant social stimulation, something shifts. The addiction to external validation—checking your phone dozens of times daily, crafting sentences for imaginary audiences, measuring worth by response rates—begins to quiet. Initially this feels like deprivation; your brain protests the withdrawal of dopamine hits that accompany likes and replies.

Yet beneath the discomfort, a deeper capacity emerges.

You begin hearing your authentic voice, the quieter one that knows what you actually believe, want, and fear, distinct from the performance voice that adjusts for audiences. This inner voice often gets drowned in company. While community is valuable, clarity frequently requires silence.

A 2017 study by Thuy-vy T. Nguyen et al., published in Personality and Social Psychology Bulletin, tracked adults engaging in voluntary solitude. Researchers found that participants who actively pursued structured contemplative practices during their alone time reported significantly increased self-knowledge and life satisfaction compared to those who simply withdrew without a framework. The key difference was not isolation itself, but how individuals purposefully engaged with it.

The participants who benefited most followed a consistent pattern: they wrote, prayed, and asked themselves directed questions rather than passively consuming content or ruminating.

To apply this approach, begin with a daily anchor practice: fifteen minutes at the same time, same place, with a journal and nothing else. No phone. No music. Just you, a pen, and one question: "What is God revealing to me right now that I've been too busy to notice?" Write whatever surfaces, even if it feels trivial or uncomfortable. This consistent space allows divine insights to emerge.

Second, end each week by reviewing what you've written. Look for patterns—recurring fears, unexpected gratitude, questions that won't resolve. These patterns reveal the curriculum of your solitude. Research on expressive writing consistently shows individuals gaining clarity on significant life decisions. Many discover, through consistent review of their reflections, recurring discomfort in certain interactions stemmed from years spent performing a role rather than genuinely living their relationships. This recognition often emerges gradually, accumulating through weeks of dedicated attention.

Third, bring one insight into action each month. Not grand shifts, but small, specific obedience.

If solitude reveals you've avoided a difficult conversation, have it. If it exposes borrowed beliefs, you do not actually hold, stop repeating them. These practices convert periods of waiting into active phases of self-discovery and growth aligned with God's Alone Plan for your transformation.

God's Presence in Our Loneliness

Consider Jesus in the wilderness, forty days fasting while Satan whispered lies about identity and power. Or David in the cave of Adullam, hiding from Saul's murderous rage while writing some of Scripture's rawest prayers. Or Joseph in an Egyptian cell, forgotten by the cupbearer he'd helped, watching years dissolve into stone walls and silence.

These weren't serene spiritual retreats.

Jesus battled genuine temptation, His humanity wrestling with shortcuts that bypassed suffering. David's psalms from those fugitive years rage against enemies and question God's timing—no sanitized devotional language, just raw desperation. Joseph endured two additional years after the cupbearer's promise, each sunrise marking another day of abandonment. Their solitude held real doubt, physical deprivation, and the terror of wondering whether God had truly disappeared.

Yet something profound happened through that wilderness time, not despite it. Jesus emerged knowing His authority with crystalline clarity. David's fugitive years forged the compassionate king who would unite Israel. Joseph's patient endurance prepared him to extend impossible forgiveness to brothers who'd sold him into slavery. Transformation occurred precisely because they remained present to God in the void, not because they escaped it quickly or performed piety for invisible audiences.

Your solitude holds the same sacred potential—not as punishment, but as divine invitation to encounter God where distractions fall away.

Recognize silence as an invitation, not rejection. When prayers feel unanswered and God seems distant, our instinct screams abandonment. Yet, a master craftsman's quiet focus isn't disinterest—it's intense concentration on the piece before him.

God's silence often signals deep work happening beneath what you can perceive. Think of it this way: emotions declare truth with conviction yet operate on incomplete information. You feel forgotten; Scripture declares He'll never leave nor forsake you. Both exist simultaneously. Which carries more weight—your fluctuating emotional weather or the character of God demonstrated across millennia?

Actively practice presence over perception through these steps: First, establish one non-negotiable daily touchpoint—morning coffee with Scripture, evening walk with spoken prayer, lunch break journaling. Consistency matters more than duration; five faithful minutes outweigh sporadic hour-long sessions. Second, document specific moments weekly where provision arrived, doors opened, or strength appeared when you had none. Third, speak truth aloud when emotions lie.

The disciples experienced this paradox acutely—Jesus asleep in the boat while the storm raged, physically present yet apparently unconcerned with their terror.

His presence doesn't depend on your perception.

Your solitude holds divine possibility, but it requires intentional practice to recognize God's presence dwelling there. Meditation, journaling, and prayer become sacred tools when approached with authenticity rather than obligation—each one transforming loneliness into profound encounter.

Begin meditation with radical simplicity. Five focused minutes outweigh thirty distracted ones. When your mind wanders during prayer—and it will—you have not failed. Simply notice the drift and gently return.

Meditation is not achieving perfect silence; it's the repeated practice of coming back. Each return strengthens your awareness of God's steady presence beneath the mental noise.

Journaling becomes powerful when you abandon religious platitudes. If you're writing "I'm grateful for blessings" on repeat, you're performing rather than encountering. Instead, write the uncomfortable truth: "I felt abandoned today when..." or "I'm angry that You haven't..." God welcomes your honest wrestling far more than your polished performances.

When these practices feel mechanical—prayers like grocery lists, journaling like obligation—stop completely for three days. Deprivation clarifies desire. Return only when genuine hunger emerges, not guilt. These are invitations to relationship, not transactions demanding immediate results.

Transformation unfolds in God's timing, not ours. As the scripture reminds us,

"To everything there is a season, and a time to every purpose under the heaven." - Ecclesiastes 3:1Ecclesiastes 3:1 (KJV):

Discovering God's presence in loneliness doesn't happen overnight—it unfolds as a sacred journey that transforms solitude into divine opportunity.

When you begin to recognize God walking beside you in your aloneness, something profound shifts. The empty room no longer feels abandoned. The quiet evening hours become invitations rather than sentences. This isn't about pretending loneliness doesn't ache—it's about discovering that even in the ache, you're not truly alone.

God meets you there, in the stillness you once feared, offering companionship that human presence cannot replicate. He sees the tears you've hidden, knows the questions you haven't voiced, and holds space for your honest wrestling with this season.

This divine presence empowers rather than pacifies. It doesn't numb the loneliness but transforms how you navigate it, replacing desperation with holy purpose.

Your solitude becomes sacred ground where God reveals truths you might have missed in the noise of companionship. Here, in this unexpected classroom, you learn who you are beyond others' definitions.

You discover strengths you didn't know you possessed and purposes you couldn't have recognized while distracted by relationship demands. What began as unwanted isolation gradually reveals itself as divinely orchestrated preparation—not punishment, but purposeful shaping for the beautiful life ahead.

Chapter 4

Building Spiritual Practice for Your Solo Life

Establishing a Daily Prayer Routine

Monks in the Egyptian desert followed a liturgical clock that divided each day into seven prayer intervals. They didn't wait for inspiration or convenient moments. They prayed at set times because they understood something most modern believers miss spiritual depth isn't built on emotion but on relentless, unglamorous repetition.

When you're alone, prayer becomes the difference between drifting and anchoring. Without the scheduled rhythms of family devotions or shared Sunday worship to carry you along, your spiritual life depends entirely on what you build in private.

Most people assume prayer flows naturally from need—that desperation or gratitude will pull them toward God when the moment requires it. They discover too late that crisis doesn't create discipline; it reveals their absence.

Consistence transforms prayer from occasional transaction into structural foundation. You pray on Tuesday morning not because you feel particularly close to God, but because Tuesday morning is when you pray. You return to the same chair, the same scripture, the same ten minutes before your day accelerates beyond your control. The content matters less initially than the showing up.

This pattern accomplishes what sporadic intensity cannot. It trains your attention to recognize God's presence outside manufactured emotion. It builds muscle memory for spiritual conversation, so when devastation or decision arrives, prayer becomes instinct rather than aspiration. Research on habit formation confirms what ancient monastics knew intuitively: repetition rewires neural pathways, making difficult practices increasingly automatic.

Your aloneness makes this both harder and more essential.

No one notices if you skip. No one's watching when you choose scrolling over silence. But that's precisely the point. What you build when no one's watching—when there's no accountability partner, no group Bible study, no spouse asking if you've prayed today—becomes the truest measure of your spiritual foundation. Consistency reveals whether your faith requires an audience.

Your prayer space isn't decoration. It's functional geography—a physical anchor point where your body learns to expect encounter with God.

Most people sabotage their prayer life before it begins by waiting for the right mood, the right words, the right emotional state. They treat prayer like inspiration, something that descends when conditions align perfectly. But neuroscience reveals what the saints have always known: environment shapes attention far more powerfully than willpower. When you pray in the same chair at the same time, your nervous system begins the shift toward presence before your mind consciously decides. Context-dependent memory means the space itself becomes a cue, triggering the state you're seeking without exhausting your limited reserves of self-control.

Choose one spot. Not the couch where you watch television. Not the bed where you scroll your phone. One location with one purpose. Keep a Bible there, a journal if that helps—nothing that requires decision-making, because complexity breeds excuses. This isn't about creating an

Instagram-worthy altar. Forget the candles and the carefully curated aesthetic.

Prioritize silence over beauty.

Put your phone in another room. Close the door. Claim this small territory back from the demands and distractions that colonize every other corner of your day. Your routine should cost you fifteen minutes you'd rather spend sleeping, scrolling, or numbing yourself with entertainment. This isn't about earning God's attention through discomfort; it's about training yourself to choose presence over convenience, to recognize that anything worth sustaining involves friction.

The sacredness doesn't come from what you place there. It comes from what you do there, repeatedly, faithfully, imperfectly. Confession without performance. Wrestling without resolution. Gratitude without pretense. Over time, that chair stops being furniture and becomes a threshold—the physical point where your solitude meets divine companionship, where showing up itself becomes prayer.

Many individuals grappling with profound loss find solace and authenticity through consistent spiritual practice. After immense grief, they often maintain a façade, reassuring friends they are "doing fine." Yet in private devotions perhaps in a quiet space each morning—the performance collapses. They weep, rage, or sit in numb silence. Through this consistent practice, a subtle shift begins: the crushing weight lifts, incrementally.

Prayer in such times is often not eloquent; for many, the only words are "I can't do this" or "Help."

Over time, individuals who felt obliterated find themselves fundamentally rebuilt. Their faith becomes deeply personal, forged in these quiet mornings when presence is chosen over performance. Research in journals like the Journal of Religion and Health and the Journal of Behavioral Medicine consistently reveals that individuals maintaining daily prayer or meditative practices for over a year experience statistically significant decreases in anxiety, improved emotional regulation, and a stronger sense of purpose. These benefits stem not from prayer eliminating difficulty, but from its capacity to cultivate internal steadiness, fostering resilience when external circumstances destabilize.

Similar transformations occur for others facing different challenges. Individuals navigating significant life transitions, like mid-life divorce, may begin contemplative practices not from crisis, but from a hollow desperation—a sense of living a script written by someone else. Their daily quiet time often becomes an archaeological process, excavating their true self beneath external expectations. Such prayer yields gradual clarification, not dramatic revelation, surfacing small, sturdy convictions that don't vanish when tested.

It transforms solitude from exile into a foundational space for self-discovery.

Incorporating Scripture into Your Solitary Moments

Scripture in solitude initiates a living conversation with God. When alone before dawn or at 2 a.m., verses become tether points that prevent emotional free fall, anchoring thoughts that spiral into catastrophe or numbness.

Receiving scripture in solitude offers an unfiltered encounter, an experience unavailable in corporate Bible study. Corporate Bible study comes filtered through group dynamics, pastor interpretation, and discussion guides. Alone, there's no buffer. Walking through actual devastation transforms Psalm 23's "valley of the shadow of death" into a raw, immediate experience. "My God, my God, why have you forsaken me?" resonates as Christ's own visceral cry of despair. These verses deliver immediate, vital sustenance, providing oxygen in the present moment.

Solitude facilitates direct dialogue with scripture. Reading Job's furious accusations offers permission to stop pretending everything's fine.

Observing Jesus withdrawing to lonely places highlights how isolation often preceded his most powerful ministry. The woman at the well, alone at noon to avoid judgment, received revelation no crowd witnessed. Paul's letters, written from prison cells, demonstrate how physical isolation can bring the deepest spiritual clarity.

This requires showing up without agenda—not hunting for answers or comfort, but opening the text and sitting with what surfaces, even if it's confusion, anger, or silence.

Building a scripture practice that actually sustains you through solitude requires more than highlighting popular verses or following someone else's reading plan. It demands something far more personal.

Start by reading without pressure to organize anything. Spend at least thirty days simply moving through scripture—Psalms work well, but so do Isaiah, John's gospel, or Paul's letters—and notice which passages make you stop. Which ones do you reread? Which ones do you copy into a journal or photograph on your phone? Frequency of return reveals genuine connection, not surface-level inspiration. A verse that pulls you back three times in one week speaks to something deep in your current reality, something that generic devotional categories might miss entirely.

After this exploration period, organize by emotional need rather than theological topic. Instead of broad categories like "hope" or "faith," create specific ones: hope when you can't feel anything, faith when God seems absent, strength for facing another empty evening.

This precision matters because scripture must address where you actually are, not where you think you should be. The Psalms themselves model this—David didn't write "trust God" when he meant "I feel abandoned and furious."

Keep your collection dynamic. What sustained you in January may feel hollow by April as your internal landscape shifts. Add verses as new needs surface. Remove ones that no longer resonate.

This isn't fickle, it's honest engagement with a living text meant to meet you wherever you are. Your personalized scripture plan becomes a field guide for navigating solitude with God, mapping the actual terrain of your journey rather than someone else's imagined path.

Reading scripture slowly reveals what speed obscures.

Most of us scan verses the way we scroll social feed consuming information, registering surface meaning, moving on. Lectio divina, the ancient practice of sacred reading, operates differently. It invites you to enter the text rather than merely observe it, creating space for God's voice to break through the noise of your thoughts.

Read the passage once for basic comprehension. Then read it again, this time listening for a single word or phrase that catches attention—not what seems most important theologically, but what actually stops you.

Circle it. Sit with it for three minutes without analysis, letting it repeat in your mind the way a song lyric does. Observe any emotions or memories that surface. This meditative space prioritizes honest response over manufactured spiritual feelings.

This practice often falters when confused with traditional Bible study. Study focuses on the text's original context—a crucial pursuit, yet distinct from meditation. Meditation seeks what God might be communicating through the text specifically to you, in your present moment and solitude. Your brain will often default to analytical mode, treating scripture like a problem to solve rather than a presence to encounter.

When you catch yourself crafting theological frameworks instead of simply sitting with the phrase, start over.

Some days produce profound insight. Most produce modest shifts slight softening toward yourself, a fragment of clarity about tomorrow, brief relief from the weight. Occasionally nothing happens at all. You might sit with Psalm 147:3 about God healing the brokenhearted and feel exactly as broken as when you started.

Empty sessions are not failures. They build the foundation for future insight, the way strength training produces results through consistent practice over weeks, even when immediate changes are imperceptible. This practice cultivates emotional resilience, often unnoticed until circumstances truly test it.

Begin with a verse already embedded in your heart, perhaps one that surfaced during morning prayer or caught your attention during meditation.

Write it at the top of a blank page. Now transform it into first person, making it yours. Philippians 4:13 becomes I can do all things through Christ who strengthens me. Not "The Bible says" or "God promises." Ownership matters. These are your declarations, speaking directly into your specific reality.

Ground each affirmation in your actual circumstances. Generic spirituality dissolves under pressure. If you're navigating post-divorce loneliness, Psalm 68:6 becomes: "God sets me in family. He's placing me where I belong, even when I eat dinner alone tonight." This concrete detail anchors the affirmation, preventing it from floating away into abstraction.

Limit yourself to three affirmations maximum. This maintains transformative focus instead of creating another spiritual checklist.

Speak to them aloud twice daily during fixed moments—morning coffee, evening routine. Whispering counts. Neuroscience shows that vocalizing affirmations strengthens their impact more than silent reading, enhancing belief formation and emotional regulation through what researchers call the production effect.

Some mornings the words will taste like lies.

You'll recite "God has not given me a spirit of fear" while anxiety physically tightens your chest. Say them anyway. The goal isn't instant certainty but practiced resistance against internal voices insisting on abandonment or unending emptiness. Affirmations don't erase those voices immediately, but they provide an alternative script during definitive darkness, building mental muscle through repetition until truth becomes an integrated reflex. Faith often develops incrementally, through small, repeated rebellions against despair that eventually stick.

Contemplative Practices for Connection and Clarity

Guided meditation offers structure when your mind resists stillness. Begin with a five-minute recording focused on God's presence—search for "Christian contemplative meditation" or "Ignatian prayer meditation." Sit upright in a chair, feet flat on the floor, hands open in your lap. Close your eyes and listen to the narrator's voice lead you through breathing, scripture, and imagery. When thoughts interrupt, they will—acknowledge them without judgment and return attention to the voice. Your mind will wander dozens of times per session. That's not failure; noticing the wandering and returning is the actual practice.

Breath prayer anchors you to God's presence throughout ordinary moments. Select a short phrase—four to eight words—that addresses your deepest need right now. "Jesus, I trust in Your timing." "Lord, fill this emptiness with Your peace." "Spirit, I am Yours and You are mine." Pair the first half with your inhale, the second with your exhale. Breathe naturally; don't force rhythm. Practice breath prayer while washing dishes, driving to work, lying awake at 3 a.m. The repetition trains your attention to return to God during moments when anxiety typically hijacks your thoughts. This isn't magical incantation—it's consistent mental redirection. After two weeks of practice, the phrase begins arising spontaneously during stress without conscious effort.

Journaling transforms internal chaos into visible patterns.

Purchase a dedicated notebook, nothing fancy, just something that opens flat. Each morning, write three pages longhand without stopping to edit, censor, or make sense. The act of writing evacuates mental clutter, allowing you to hear what lies underneath. Complain, question, rage, wonder—whatever surfaces. Date each entry.

Within thirty days, flip back and read the earliest pages. You'll notice recurring themes you couldn't see while living inside them: persistent fears masquerading as different concerns, God's faithfulness you forgot three days later, gradual shifts in perspective you didn't register happening. This practice clears your mind rather than merely recording events, it reveals the divine whispers buried beneath the noise.

Combine these practices through a weekly contemplative hour. Saturday morning or Sunday evening, eliminate distractions completely. Begin with ten minutes of guided meditation. Transition to fifteen minutes reading scripture slowly—one psalm, one gospel passage. Write for twenty minutes responding to whatever the text surfaced: questions, resistance, memories, gratitude.

Close with ten minutes of breath prayer, letting the phrase carry you back into presence. Approach this hour as cultivation, distinct from typical productivity goals. Some weeks will feel profound. Most will feel ordinary. Both matter equally, because consistency builds the spiritual muscle that sustains you through every season.

Your sacred space doesn't require perfection. It requires intention.

This isn't about acquiring the right cushion, the perfect lighting, or religiously symbolic décor that looks borrowed from someone else's spiritual journey. Your sacred space needs only one essential quality: consistent association. A corner of your bedroom, a chair by the window, even a specific spot on your couch—anywhere your mind learns to recognize as the threshold between the noise of daily life and the presence of God.

Over time, simply entering this space will signal your entire being to settle, to open, to listen. The physical anchor becomes a bridge to divine encounter, a geography of the soul that remains steady when everything else shifts.

Start by choosing a location that feels naturally quiet, somewhere you can realistically access without significant disruption to your routine. Mornings before the world makes demands, evenings after obligations release their grip, even midday moments stolen from the relentless forward momentum. The timing matters less than the consistency.

Your nervous system requires repetition to build new pathways, and your spirit needs the rhythm of returning again and again to the same meeting place.

Prepare your space with simple intentions. Remove distraction silence your phone, clear away clutter that fragments your attention. You might include a candle, scripture, and a journal, but these are invitations rather than requirements. The sacred emerges not from objects but from your willingness to show up, to create deliberate separation from productivity and performance, to practice the vulnerable art of simply being present before God.

Expect resistance. Your mind will generate urgent tasks the moment you sit down, suddenly convinced that emails require immediate response or household projects demand attention this very second.

This isn't coincidence—stillness threatens the mechanisms you've built to avoid pain, so your psyche manufactures emergencies to pull you back into motion. Recognize this pattern without judgment, then choose presence anyway.

Write down the intrusive thoughts if necessary, acknowledging them without surrendering to them. The resistance eventually diminishes, though it never disappears completely. Learning to sit with it builds the contemplative muscle that transforms your entire spiritual life.

Chapter 5

Healing From the Events That Led to Your Aloneness

Acknowledging Your Pain and Loss

Pain doesn't announce itself politely. It arrives with the force of a semi-truck—the moment divorce papers are signed, the instant a hospital room goes silent, the night you realize the loneliness isn't temporary. One woman described it as waking up to find her entire skeleton had been replaced overnight; everything looked the same from the outside, but internally, nothing worked the way it used to.

Most of us respond to this invasion by doing what feels natural: we minimize it. We tell ourselves it could be worse. We compare our grief to someone else's tragedy and decide ours doesn't qualify.

We keep working, keep smiling at the grocery store, keep showing up to church with carefully constructed answers about how we're doing. This isn't strength—it's self-abandonment, a refusal to acknowledge what's real.

Your pain has depth, and that depth demands acknowledgment. Losing a marriage involves more than the absence of a person; it's the collapse of a built future, the shedding of a long-held identity, the disruption of daily rituals that gave shape to your weeks.

The death of a spouse creates an overwhelming absence, dismantling the architecture of your entire life. These losses burrow into layers you didn't know existed: the physical, where your body literally aches; the social, where invitations dry up and friendships shift; the spiritual, where God feels distant; the practical, where simple decisions become overwhelming; the existential, where you wonder who am I without them?

Healing cannot begin until you stop pretending the wound is smaller than it is.

Unspoken pain festers in darkness. It distorts your perspective, crafting an unreliable narrative fueled by shame and isolation that keeps you bound.

Sharing what happened with another human being, someone who can absorb its weight without flinching—changes everything. Grief counseling studies from organizations like the Hospice Foundation of America reveal a common pattern: individuals finally articulating details previously deemed too shameful or irrational often experience profound breakthroughs.

One bereaved parent, after months of silence, confessed to a trusted friend the overwhelming guilt over not saying "I love you" on the morning of their child's sudden death. This raw admission, met with empathy rather than platitudes, allowed them to confront the distorted narrative of self-blame. It marked a crucial step away from isolation toward healing.

Such witnessing validates your private anguish.

It confirms that your experience was real and significant. Your loss gains external recognition; someone else now understands its specific gravity. This acknowledgment alone can begin to lift the burden you've carried in solitude, replacing isolation with the sacred gift of being truly seen.

Honest sharing reveals something equally powerful: you are not uniquely broken. Others have navigated similar devastation, experiencing the same irrational guilt, disorienting anger, and fear that the pain will never end. Your vulnerability creates space for connection, transforming your story from a source of shame into a bridge toward community and support.

Your story offers a lifeline to others still isolated by silence. A firsthand account of survival after profound loss provides permission for them to acknowledge their own struggles and cease pretense. This redemptive impact begins with sharing your unedited reality with just one trustworthy person.

Pain and faith collide most violently when loss feels incompatible with divine love.

The chasm between theological certainty and lived devastation paralyzes many believers. They grapple with reconciling a benevolent God with a shattered life. While told that "all things work together for good," it's impossible to fathom what good emerges from burying a spouse or watching decades of marriage dissolve. This disconnect feels unbearable.

Some abandon faith entirely, convinced that suffering proves God's absence. Others perform belief while privately seething, their prayers hollow recitations masking profound doubt.

Faith was never meant to erase grief.

Scripture offers no tidy explanation for suffering. Job received no answer to his anguished questions, only God's overwhelming presence. Jesus wept at Lazarus's tomb despite knowing resurrection was imminent. David's psalms swing wildly between trust and accusation, sometimes within the same verse. Such expressions reveal faith robust enough to contain fury, confusion, and sorrow without collapsing.

Pain deepens your capacity for divine purpose. The suffering that seems to separate you from God can become the very ground for authentic relationship. While pain itself holds no redemptive power, honestly confronting it—bringing unfiltered anguish directly to God rather than sanitizing it—forges a profound intimacy that superficial faith cannot replicate.

The Role of Faith in the Healing Process

Faith becomes functional when suffering transforms belief from intellectual proposition into practiced refuge. When grief splits open your world, Scripture stops being Sunday-morning decoration and becomes oxygen at 3 a.m.—the single tether preventing complete unraveling.

Comfort arrives not as explanation but as presence. God never promised to clarify why your spouse died or your marriage disintegrated. Faith offers endurance, rather than resolution. You wake shattered, open Psalm 34, and find "The Lord is close to the brokenhearted" speaks directly to your Tuesday morning, when getting out of bed feels impossible. This isn't abstract theology—it's survival.

Faith provides structure when internal architecture collapses. Prayer becomes the framework holding fragmented days together. Worship reorients attention beyond immediate devastation. Community offers witness when you cannot carry weight alone. The consistent presence of a faith community or the predictable cadence of liturgy acts as a vital anchor during profound loss, offering necessary framework even when spiritual feelings are absent.

Trusting God's plan amid catastrophic loss sounds like cruel abstraction until you recognize it doesn't mean approving what happened.

It means believing devastation isn't the final word. Joseph didn't deserve enslavement, yet Genesis records him later acknowledging divine purpose woven through injustice. Ruth's widowhood was genuine tragedy, not disguised blessing—but faithfulness within that tragedy positioned her within redemptive lineage she couldn't foresee. These stories don't diminish pain; they reveal that God works through brokenness, not around it.

The transformative power emerges slowly. Comfort doesn't erase grief; instead, it permits you to continue existing while carrying it. Some mornings that whisper is all that sustains you.

Maria's story cuts to the heart of what surrender actually means. After her husband's sudden death, she spent eighteen months performing grief—attending support groups, journaling obsessively, reading every recommended devotional—while internally resisting the one truth everyone kept offering: that she needed to surrender control.

She'd constructed elaborate plans for recovering normalcy. Timelines for when sadness should diminish. Strategies for managing her children's emotions. Detailed projections of financial stability. Each plan represented her attempt to impose order on chaos, to wrestle devastation into something manageable through sheer force of will.

The breakthrough arrived during a particularly brutal anniversary week when every strategy failed simultaneously.

Exhausted from fighting, she finally prayed for words she'd avoided: "I can't do this. You take it." Not poetic. Not profound. Just honest capitulation born from desperation. That simple prayer changed everything. The crushing responsibility of orchestrating her own healing lifted.

She stopped interrogating every emotional fluctuation as evidence of progress or failure. When her son struggled, she prayed instead of panic-planning. When finances tightened, she asked for help rather than manufacturing solutions through willpower alone.

Here's what many misunderstand about surrendering to God's will: it doesn't mean passivity. Maria continued to parent, work, and make decisions. She simply abandoned the exhausting pretense that her relentless effort could force healing on her preferred schedule. Yielding to God's timeline created space for genuine transformation—the kind that emerges when we stop blocking it with our own agendas.

Research on grief resilience confirms what faith has always known: acceptance marks the inflection point where genuine healing begins. When we yield to the process rather than fighting it, divine grace operates in ways our carefully orchestrated plans often obstruct.

Surrender reveals a path forward, but most people stall at the question of how. Faith integration sounds spiritually correct until Monday morning arrives and the gap between theological belief and lived experience yawns impossibly wide.

Start with morning reorientation—not because mornings possess magical properties, but because they arrive before chaos demands your attention. Before checking your phone, speak one sentence aloud: a verse, a truth about God's presence, even just "You are here with me."

Your voice in the empty room becomes tangible rebellion against the lie that you navigate this alone. Consistency matters more than duration. Ninety seconds of genuine connection outweighs thirty minutes of distracted performance.

Physical spaces anchor spiritual practice in ways willpower cannot sustain. Designate one specific chair, corner, or spot outdoors as your meeting place with God. Not your bed, where sleep blurs boundaries. Not your desk, contaminated by work stress. Somewhere your body learns to expect divine encounter. When grief ambushes you at 3 p.m., that geography becomes refuge—muscle memory guiding you toward the place where God has consistently met you before.

Yet even well-designed practices fail when circumstances intensify.

After a job loss or the sudden illness of a loved one, established morning routines often shatter. A person who faithfully began their day with quiet reflection for months might find themselves staring at their designated spot, feeling profound emptiness. Their fifteen-minute practice becomes a cruel reminder of normalcy lost, yielding only hollow words.

The once-sacred chair transforms into a symbol of spiritual struggle, leading them to abandon the routine entirely, convinced it never truly worked. This common experience illustrates what sustainable practice actually requires: returning after collapse.

Faith disciplines function like physical therapy after injury—missing sessions happens, but abandoning rehabilitation guarantees permanent dysfunction. The practice itself becomes healing, regardless of how it feels in the moment. Choose the chair again after weeks of absence. Speak truth aloud even when it tastes like ash.

Faith doesn't just comfort rebuilds. When your world collapses, belief becomes the blueprint for reconstruction, transforming wreckage into foundation.

This transformation requires three specific weekly practices, not vague spiritual intentions. These disciplines create structural integrity that holds when feelings fail.

First, the Sunday inventory. Every Sunday evening, spend twenty minutes with a notebook answering three questions: Where did I encounter God this week? Where did I avoid Him?

What single truth do I need to carry forward? Write by hand—the slower pace forces honesty your racing thoughts would skip. This written record provides visible proof that faith persisted through your hardest seasons. When doubt whispers that God abandoned you, flip backward through pages proving otherwise.

Second, intercessory anchoring. Choose two specific people experiencing struggle and pray for them by name every Tuesday and

Thursday. Focus on concrete requests tied to their actual circumstances. This practice demolishes the isolation convincing you that suffering is solitary. Your faith strengthens as you exercise it on behalf of others, redirecting focus outward when introspection becomes quicksand.

Third, establish one non-negotiable Sabbath boundary. Even if a full day of rest isn't feasible, protect one hour where productivity has no claim. Turn off your phone. Take a walk with no destination. Sit doing nothing efficiently. This hour cultivates receptivity over achievement, weekly demonstrating that your worth isn't tethered to output.

These three rhythms—Sunday inventory, Tuesday-Thursday intercession, one Sabbath hour—create stability independent of emotional weather. Their value lies not in immediate transformation, but in repetition that builds neural pathways carrying you through times when emotions falter entirely.

Moving Forward: Strategies for Emotional Resilience

Name three emotions you've felt in the last forty-eight hours. Not the ones you admit at church or describe to friends—the actual ones that surface when you're brushing your teeth or waiting at a stoplight.

Write them down. Anger, numbness, shame, unexpected joy, resentment, relief. Whatever appeared. Most people can't do this exercise without pausing. We've learned to dismiss emotions before they fully register, categorizing them as appropriate or problematic before acknowledging they exist. Healing requires reversing this reflex.

Create what therapists call an emotional elaborate, just a page where you record feelings as they surface throughout one week. Set phone reminders at 10 a.m., 3 p.m., and 8 p.m. When the alarm sounds, stop and identify: What am I feeling right now? One word is sufficient. You're not analyzing or justifying, just noticing. By Friday, patterns emerge.

You discover anger arrives every afternoon around 2:30, or grief hits hardest Sunday mornings, or anxiety spikes when you open email. These consistent observations provide critical information for your body communicates, often despite your mind's prior insistence that everything was fine.

Next, practice verbal acknowledgment without immediately solving. Standing in your designated space, speak one difficult emotion aloud to God: "I feel furious that this happened." Then stop. Don't rush to "but I know You have a plan" or "help me not feel this way." Let the statement exist unedited for thirty seconds. Your throat might tighten. That's normal. You're building tolerance for truth.

For emotions you can't name, use the body as translator. Scan from head to feet: Where do I feel tightness? Heaviness? Emptiness? Chest constriction often signals anxiety, jaw tension indicates anger, and stomach hollowness frequently accompanies grief. Ask: If this sensation could speak, what would it say? Write whatever emerges without censoring.

Finally, establish one weekly practice specifically for difficult emotions. Saturday morning, sit with your journal and complete this sentence five times: "Something I haven't let myself feel is..." Then choose one and pray it raw: "God, I'm terrified I'll always be alone." No Scripture chaser, no theological correction. Just honest offering.

Acknowledgment doesn't resolve pain. It stops the exhausting pretense that creates a second suffering layered over the first.

These practices—naming emotions, creating rhythms, speaking truth aloud, establishing sacred space—form the infrastructure that holds you when feelings don't. They're not dramatic.

Most days they won't feel like breakthroughs.

That's precisely why they work.

Resilience isn't built through mountaintop moments but through unglamorous repetition on ordinary Tuesdays when nothing feels different and you show up anyway. The emotion log becomes reflex. Morning reorientation happens before coffee. Your designated chair trains your nervous system to expect God's presence even when you can't sense it.

These tools teach you to navigate aloneness without drowning, to carry grief without it consuming everything, and to encounter God even when the scaffolding of community and routine has collapsed. You're learning what the desert fathers discovered: spiritual depth requires structure independent of inspiration.

When loss strips away external validation, borrowed beliefs, and others' interpretations, these practices reveal what authentic faith remains. They become the bedrock that doesn't shift when relationships eventually return, the self-knowledge that prevents you from loving out of desperation or serving because you need applause.

Some weeks you'll forget entirely. You'll skip journaling for nine days straight, abandon the emotion log, pray only desperate fragments at stoplights.

Perfection isn't the point. Progress compounds through returning after collapse, not through flawless execution.

You've identified specific wounds requiring grief rather than performance, established practices that acknowledge pain without being consumed by it, and built tangible rhythms connecting theological belief to 3 a.m. reality. Healing begins through active participation, as small, concrete choices accumulate into transformation.

With this foundation built, you are now prepared to move these internal shifts outward—to navigate the complicated, necessary work of rebuilding connection without losing the ground you've gained alone.

Chapter 6

Discovering and Developing Your Authentic Self

The Freedom of Solitude: A Gateway to Self-Discovery

Most people tolerate solitude. Some endure it.

A rare few understand that it contains possibilities unavailable anywhere else. The distinction matters profoundly, because our default interpretation of being alone has been shaped by forces that profit from our discomfort. From childhood forward, we've absorbed a relentless message: solitary time signals something broken.

Birthday parties measure social success by headcount. College applications valorize leadership and team involvement. Dating culture pathologizes those who eat dinner alone. The underlying assumption remains constant—aloneness equals deficiency.

This conditioning runs deeper than conscious belief. Neuroscientist John Cacioppo's research revealed that chronic perception of social isolation triggers the same threat response as physical danger, flooding the body with cortisol and adrenaline. Your nervous system, trained by cultural messaging, interprets an empty Saturday evening as evidence of failure requiring immediate correction.

But this physiological threat response is a consequence of cultural training, not an objective indicator of danger inherent in solitude.

A conscious separation of the experience of being alone from these ingrained cultural narratives is necessary for true engagement with solitude. The discomfort you feel in silence? It signals the surfacing of crucial internal dialogue. Solitary periods provide a powerful environment for deep self-reflection—an opportunity frequently missed amidst constant external engagement. When approached with active inquiry, these moments reveal specific and deeply personal insights about who you truly are.

Self-discovery doesn't happen by accident. It requires deliberate examination of your inner world, your values, desires, fears, the patterns that shape your days—free from the distorting lens of others' expectations. This sacred work demands specific tools, not merely good intentions.

Three practices form the foundation of authentic self-discovery: journaling, structured reflection, and creative expression. Each serves a distinct purpose in revealing who you truly are beneath the layers of performance and protection you've built over time.

Journaling creates a record of thoughts you cannot perceive in real time. Writing by hand slows your mind enough to notice what you actually think versus what you believe you should think. Beginning with ten minutes of unfiltered stream-of-consciousness writing each morning—no editing, no concern for beauty or coherence.

You're not crafting literature; you're capturing truth. Over weeks, patterns appear like constellations: specific fears mentioned across multiple entries, consistent sources of resentment, desires you've repeatedly dismissed as impractical or selfish.

Structured reflection transforms raw journaling into genuine insight. Once weekly, answer three essential questions: What drained my energy this week? What energized me? Where did I compromise my true preferences to avoid conflict or judgment? These prompts expose the gap between your performed self and your authentic self—the version God created you to be.

Creative expression functions differently than analysis. Painting, writing fiction, playing music, building something with your hands—these activities bypass the rational gatekeepers that censor uncomfortable truths. You discover what truly matters not through logical deduction but by noticing what captures your attention when you're not trying to prove anything or please anyone.

These tools work through accumulation, not sudden epiphany. Consistency matters far more than intensity. Fifteen minutes of journaling twice weekly outperforms sporadic marathon sessions because the practice itself rewires how you process experience, training you to notice patterns as they unfold rather than only in retrospect.

Martha Beck arrived at Harvard with a Ph.D. and all the conventional markers of success, yet she felt profoundly hollow inside. She had built her entire life around external expectations—what she should be, not who

Practical Strategies for Personal Growth During Alone Time

Journaling creates a physical record of thoughts that otherwise evaporate the moment you think them. When anxiety spirals or grief resurfaces, the mind convinces you that this feeling is unprecedented, permanent, unbearable. A journal proves otherwise. Last month's entry reveals you felt identical despair—and survived it.

Three weeks ago, you wrote the same worry about your finances, your purpose, your capacity to rebuild. The pattern becomes visible only when documented. Most people approach journaling incorrectly, treating blank pages as confessionals for dramatic revelations. Effective journaling requires less poetry, more precision.

Write what actually happened today, not what it meant. "Declined lunch invitation from Maria. Felt relief, then guilt" holds more useful data than "I'm struggling with social connections." The first entry gives you something concrete to examine: Why relief? What specifically triggered the guilt? Was it about Maria, or about violating an internalized rule that isolated people must accept every invitation? Over weeks, these factual entries reveal unconscious patterns.

You discover you feel most peaceful between 6 and 8 a.m., that phone conversations drain you while emails don't, that you've mentioned your late husband's golf clubs in seven separate entries without addressing them directly. These patterns point toward truths your conscious mind hasn't acknowledged.

Perhaps mornings are when God speaks most clearly to you. Perhaps you need written processing time before verbal interaction. Perhaps those golf clubs in the garage represent unfinished grief you've been sidestepping.

Journaling reveals a quiet recognition: your Thursday irritability correlates with skipping prayer for three days running, or every entry mentioning your sister holds resentment you've never named aloud.

Your solitude holds untapped potential for remarkable transformation—if you choose to invest in yourself rather than simply endure the quiet. Learning new skills and exploring hobbies during your alone season isn't about filling empty hours. It's about discovering capacities you never knew existed, building competence that fuels confidence, and creating tangible evidence that you're moving forward, not standing still.

Consider the practical power of skill-building. When you learn a new language, master photography, or develop cooking expertise, you're not just acquiring knowledge.

You're proving to yourself that growth remains possible, that your story isn't over, that this season of solitude can produce something beautiful and lasting. Each new capability becomes a building block of your authentic identity—not who others expected you to be, but who you're genuinely becoming.

Start with what genuinely sparks your curiosity, not what impresses others.

The investment doesn't require dramatic commitments or expensive equipment. Online courses, library resources, and community workshops offer accessible pathways.

What matters is consistent engagement with something that challenges and energizes you. Perhaps you've always wondered about woodworking, photography, or playing guitar. Maybe gardening appeals to your desire to nurture growth, or painting offers an outlet for emotions words cannot capture. Your alone time becomes sacred space when you dedicate it to pursuits that genuinely reflect your interests rather than obligations.

This isn't escapism—it's purposeful cultivation of the person God designed you to be. Each skill mastered, each hobby explored, each creative risk taken writes a new chapter in your story of faithful independence and thriving solo life.

Continuous learning requires infrastructure, not just enthusiasm. Your initial excitement about mastering Italian or understanding quantum physics will fade—usually around week three, when novelty gives way to the grinding repetition that actually rewires your brain.

This isn't a character flaw. It's neuroscience. New behaviors demand roughly 66 days of consistent practice before they become automatic, and those weeks feel uncomfortable before they feel natural.

Build accountability before inspiration evaporates.

Prepay for that online course so abandoning it costs you money. Schedule learning sessions like doctor's appointments—non-negotiable blocks in your calendar. Tell a specific person what you're studying and ask them to check your progress next month. These external structures endure when feelings don't. They create friction against quitting that your future self, tired and doubting, will grudgingly appreciate.

But recognize when learning becomes avoidance. If you're accumulating certifications to paper over deeper vocational misalignment, studying subjects that impress others rather than energize you, or endlessly preparing instead of ever applying—pause.

Learning becomes sophisticated procrastination when it distracts from necessary grief or substitutes for feared human connection. Productive challenge leaves you tired but fuller; compulsive distraction leaves you exhausted and hollow.

Some seasons demand consolidation, not expansion. During acute loss or clinical depression, attempting complex skill acquisition can overwhelm already depleted resources. Permission to pause matters as much as encouragement to begin.

Eventually, you must close the tutorial and take the photograph, stop reading about prayer and actually pray. Knowledge without implementation builds impressive libraries but doesn't transform your actual life.

Identify one dormant creative project—not the entire graveyard of abandoned dreams, but a single endeavor that keeps circling back to your thoughts. That novel outline you tucked away three years ago.

The pottery wheel collecting dust in the garage. The garden space you've imagined transforming a hundred times. Select what calls to you in quiet moments, not what sounds impressive to others.

Schedule two specific hours this Saturday. Write it in your calendar with the project's name, making it as non-negotiable as a doctor's appointment.

During that first session, create something tangible, however flawed. Write five hundred messy words that finally exist beyond your imagination. Sketch three imperfect versions of what you've been picturing. Build that birdhouse frame even if the corners sit crooked.

Done always triumph over perfect because completion teaches what endless planning cannot. You'll learn that watercolors bleed differently than you expected that your character's voice surprises you on paper, that cedar splits cleaner than pine. These discoveries emerge only through doing, never through research.

Establish your weekly rhythm before inspiration evaporates—same day, same time, same commitment. Creative practice mirrors prayer: those rare sessions when inspiration flows matter less than the dozens when you simply showed up.

Repetition carves neural pathways, transforming awkward attempts into natural expressions. That first paragraph demands forty minutes of blank-page starting; six weeks later, your hands move before doubt can interrupt.

Around week four, expect resistance to surface—this discomfort signals growth, not failure.

The project itself becomes your teacher, revealing reserves of patience you didn't know you possessed and preferences you couldn't have named without testing them against reality. Through creative expression, you're not just making art; you're discovering who God created you to be when nobody's watching.

Investing in Yourself: Turning Solitude into Opportunity

Within seventy-two hours of reading this, choose one specific skill that genuinely addresses where you are right now. Not something that sounds impressive. Not something everyone else is learning. Choose your thing—photography, Spanish, financial planning, watercolor painting, coding, woodworking. Write down exactly why these matters to you, in your own words, for your own reasons.

Then make it cost something.

Register for a course with a non-refundable deposit. Tell three people your specific goal and when you report progress. Block recurring calendar appointments for learning sessions and treat them like doctor's appointments—because investing in your growth deserves that level of commitment. Accountability transforms vague intentions into tangible commitments.

The first session will likely feel exhilarating. The tenth session, when the material gets tedious and your motivation wanes, reveals whether you're truly committed to growth or just chasing the feeling of starting something new.

Create a dedicated learning space with everything ready—charged laptop, textbooks, notebooks, whatever you need within arm's reach. Eliminate every excuse. You should be able to begin immediately, without searching for supplies or making decisions. Keep a simple learning journal tracking what works: when you retain information best, which teaching styles click, where you hit resistance. After two weeks, review your patterns and adjust accordingly. This isn't bureaucracy; it's self-knowledge.

Set bi-weekly completion checkpoints. Finish something tangible, complete a module, translate a passage, edit a photo series, build a functional spreadsheet, paint an actual canvas. Completion, unlike endless consumption, gives you evidence. It proves that your solitude is producing lasting growth, not just filling time.

But watch for the trap: learning as sophisticated avoidance. If you're collecting certificates without applying anything, studying for external validation, or endlessly preparing instead of practicing, stop. Ask yourself honestly whether you’re learning serves genuine growth or merely cushions you from the discomfort of actually doing something with what you know.

Some seasons require consolidation rather than acquisition. Close the tutorial. Take the photograph. Have a conversation. Write the first chapter. Learning without application becomes intellectual entertainment—just as faith without work remains theoretical. God refines you for purpose, and purpose requires stepping beyond study into uncertain practice, where your knowledge meets reality and transforms into wisdom.

Passion projects aren't hobbies you fit into spare moments—they're lifelines anchoring you to who you're becoming. When you invest creative energy into something purely for your own fulfillment, unburdened by anyone else's expectations or approval, you're doing more than filling time. You're reclaiming sovereignty over your inner world. That dusty canvas in your closet, the novel outline you revisit at midnight, the garden you've sketched but never planted—these aren't failures to act. They're invitations waiting for your yes.

Creative expression fundamentally changes how solitude feels. It focuses on scattered attention when your thoughts spin. It gives shape to emotions too tangled for words. It connects abstract worry to something you can touch, mold, transform. Neuroscience confirms this: creative acts activate your brain's reward system and strengthen areas tied to self-reflection, building psychological resilience from the inside out. A 2017 study in the Journal of the American Academy of Psychiatry and the Law demonstrated that visual art creation reduces stress and improves neural connectivity in older adults—tangible proof that making something matters more than consuming it.

When you shape raw materials into something new, you're proving to yourself that your choices hold power. That beauty can emerge from your hands.

But fulfillment demands action, not endless preparation. Stop researching the perfect watercolor set. Stop curating inspiration boards. Stop waiting for ideal conditions that will never arrive. Block two non-negotiable hours this week and begin creating, even badly. Five clumsy pots teach more than fifty pottery tutorials ever could. Your first attempts will disappoint you—create them anyway.

Consistency unlocks depth. Around your fourth session, when novelty fades and the urge to quit whispers loud, something shifts. The brush feels less foreign. The chord progression flows instead of trips. You've stopped performing and started inhabiting the work. This transformation—from awkward imitation to genuine engagement—is when solitude stops feeling empty and becomes fertile ground.

Pay attention to what you create when no one's watching. It maps your authentic self with precision that introspection often misses, revealing truths your creative choices make visible.

Chapter 7

Building Financial Security and Independence

Understanding Financial Anxiety in Solitude

Financial anxiety hits differently when you're alone, no second income to soften a layoff, no partner to brainstorm budget cuts over dinner, no one to reassure you that the spreadsheet catastrophizing at 3 a.m. might be overblown. The numbers become existential in ways they never were when shared.

For most people living solo, financial fear isn't primarily about actual insolvency. It's about the narrative underneath: If I can't make this work financially, it proves I'm fundamentally incapable. This conflation—collapsing temporary circumstance into permanent identity—turns practical challenges into a verdict on your worth.

A surprise car repair swiftly escalates from a budget adjustment to perceived personal failure, a catastrophic error, or proof you can't handle what others manage effortlessly.

These stories typically root in childhood messages about money and self-sufficiency. Perhaps you watched a parent panic over bills, internalizing that financial struggle equals personal failure. Maybe your family equated wealth with virtue, scarcity with moral deficiency. Or you absorbed gendered expectations—men provide, women depend—creating shame when reality doesn't conform.

Financial anxiety in solitude feeds on silence. When no one witnesses your budget, sees your account balance, or knows you're eating rice and beans the week before payday, the internal narrative runs unchecked. The spreadsheet becomes mirror, and what it reflects feels like truth about who you fundamentally are rather than where you currently stand.

Financial fear loses its power when you drag it into the light. Those midnight anxieties—the catastrophic scenarios, the vague sense of drowning—they shrink when you force them onto paper. Problems that multiply in darkness become manageable when named.

Start with an honest assessment of where you actually stand, not the disaster story your anxiety whispers at 3 a.m. Document every income source, every fixed expense, every debt with its interest rate. Write it by hand if you can—there's something about physically forming the numbers that disrupts the endless mental loop and forces precision where estimation breeds terror.

This isn't about creating an impressive budget or a color-coded spreadsheet worthy of sharing. This is about establishing truth so your mind stops inventing fiction.

When you externalize your financial reality, something shifts. Vague anxiety transforms into specific problems with identifiable solutions. You're no longer "bad with money"—you discover three forgotten subscriptions draining $47 monthly. You're not facing some inherent "financial incompetence"—you're looking at a credit card charging 23% interest that could be refinanced. The crushing weight of inadequacy becomes a numbered list of actions. Call the utility company about a payment plan. Research balance transfer options. Cancel that service you never use.

Faith doesn't promise magical provision, but it does offer something more sustainable: a relocated sense of identity. Scripture addresses anxiety about provision not by dismissing practical concerns, but by insisting your worth extends beyond your bank balance. You are not what you own. You are not what you owe.

Before opening those bills, pray for clarity to see the truth of your situation and courage to face it without shame.

Then take the next right step, no matter how small.

Nobody navigates financial fear alone by accident. You require deliberate connections with people who understand the specific terror of opening bills when you're managing a household solo.

Research consistently demonstrates that financial stress intensifies in isolation. The Federal Reserve's Report on the Economic Well-Being of U.S. Households consistently highlights widespread financial anxiety, and strong social support significantly mitigates stress and fosters more adaptive financial decision-making. Your brain under financial stress literally functions differently—the prefrontal cortex responsible for rational planning goes offline while the amygdala screams danger. This is a biological reality, not a personal failing.

Faith communities offer infrastructure secular society rarely provides: practical resource-sharing that predates government safety nets by millennia. Early church communities in Acts pooled resources so aggressively that "there were no needy persons among them"—not through state programs, but through believers who sold property to ensure others ate. Modern iterations look less dramatic but equally practical: church benevolence funds for unexpected car repairs, meal rotations during job transitions, childcare exchanges that save hundreds monthly, and critically, financial peace groups where discussing money stops being shameful.

Yet many believers sit silently in pews, convinced asking for help reveals failure rather than faith.

God designed the body of Christ with interdependence woven through every metaphor—when one part suffers, the whole body responds. Seeking support aligns with divine provision, as God frequently works through the hands of His people. Find one trustworthy person who will ask the uncomfortable questions about your budget. Join a faith-based financial group. Name your actual need.

Community doesn't eliminate financial anxiety, but it prevents the catastrophic thinking that solitude breeds.

Creating a Sustainable Financial Plan

Financial awareness begins with something deceptively simple: writing down what you actually earn and spend each month, not what you think you should earn or wish you spent.

Most people resist this because they're afraid of what they'll discover. But vague awareness—the sense that you're "probably overspending" or "should be saving more"—creates far more anxiety than concrete numbers ever could. Many people fear their discretionary spending is out of control. Yet, upon tracking, they discover their actual monthly spending on categories like dining out or entertainment is a manageable $300-$500, a figure often aligned with their income and priorities, not reckless excess. This clarity dissolves self-judgment, replacing it with objective understanding.

Start with one month of raw data.

Track every dollar that comes in: salary, freelance payments, child support, that $20 your sister repaid. Then track every dollar out: rent, utilities, groceries, the coffee you grabbed Tuesday morning, the streaming service you forgot you had. Use whatever method you'll actually maintain—a notebook, a spreadsheet, an app—but make it visible. This initial stage is purely about establishing a factual baseline, not about judgment or perfection.

Within two weeks, patterns emerge that your anxious mind obscured. You'll spot the subscription charging $12.99 monthly for a service you haven't used since 2022. You'll notice you spend $80 weekly eating out not because you're careless, but because you work ten-hour days and arrive home exhausted. These concrete insights become the foundation for meaningful change, transforming financial fog into divine clarity.

For many navigating significant life transitions, confronting personal finances can feel overwhelming. Perhaps you've spent eighteen months avoiding your bank statements after a profound loss, paying bills reactively, transferring money when accounts run low, living in that perpetual low-grade panic about whether enough exists. Sometimes fear feels safer than facing the numbers.

When you finally map out a complete budget, you expect catastrophe—proof you cannot survive alone. What emerges instead is often revelation. A forgotten life insurance payout surfaces. Those nebulous monthly expenses of "too much" resolve into an actual $3,400. You discover $340 flowing to grandchildren each month—generous, yes, but intentional, reflecting a value you want to preserve. Within weeks of seeing real numbers, those 3 a.m. financial terrors often subside, not because circumstances have dramatically changed, but because vague dread has transformed into specific, manageable truth.

Research published in the Journal of Financial Therapy confirms what you might experience: individuals who actively budget report significantly lower financial anxiety than those with similar incomes who only mentally track spending. Externalizing financial reality—moving it from rumination to documentation—activates problem-solving regions rather than fear centers.

A purposeful budget doesn't restrict your life. It reveals where your money currently goes, then asks whether that aligns with what matters most. When you discover $95 monthly on convenience foods but can't afford the woodworking class you've wanted, you're not learning you're irresponsible.

You're learning your spending doesn't yet match your actual priorities.

Emergency funds provide concrete financial protection, transforming a flat tire from a month-derailing catastrophe into a Tuesday inconvenience. Financial experts typically recommend three to six months of expenses, but this target can feel overwhelming when you're navigating month-to-month stability alone.

Start with $500.

This amount covers most immediate crises: urgent prescriptions, minor car repairs, water heater failures on Saturday nights. Once $500 sits in a separate account—physically distant from your checking, requiring deliberate transfer—your sleep improves. You stop bargaining with fate when the check engine light appears. You breathe differently knowing you've prepared for life's inevitable surprises.

Automatic transfers often fail by month three, when initial enthusiasm fades and that $50 weekly deposit feels like deprivation rather than divine protection. The money vanishes into an account whose growth you never witness.

Manual transfers work better for many. Every payday, physically move money and watch your balance climb. Some prefer cash envelopes—labeling one "Emergency" and watching bills accumulate creates visceral security no app notification can replicate. Others need friction removed entirely, automating transfers the moment income arrives, before spending decisions begin. You're not building wealth yet; you're building capacity to absorb shock without catastrophizing—which is its own form of abundance. This foundation makes every subsequent financial decision less desperate, because one unexpected expense no longer threatens to unravel everything you've built alone.

Once emergencies no longer dictate your finances, money can begin working for you—not through complex schemes, but through the quiet power of compound time.

Many solo adults fear investing, seeing it as exclusive territory requiring vast capital or insider knowledge. Yet its core principle is beautifully simple: consistent contributions over time. Employer-sponsored retirement accounts like 401(k)s or 403(b)s automatically deduct pre-tax dollars from each paycheck. Employer matching offers an immediate, guaranteed return on your investment; failing to contribute means refusing free money that's already yours.

Start small. Even 3% of your income, faithfully deposited, compounds over decades into substantial security.

Target-date funds adjust risk automatically as you age, requiring only that you select an approximate retirement year. This approach relies on long-term economic growth through patient, repeated deposits—not stock trading or market timing. Outside employer plans, low-cost index funds available through platforms like Vanguard or Fidelity require no special expertise. They spread risk across hundreds of companies, tracking overall market performance rather than individual stock volatility.

The process is refreshingly straightforward: open an account, link your bank, schedule modest monthly transfers of $25, $50, or $100. Review quarterly, not daily, to build perspective and resist panic during market fluctuations. This isn't about getting rich quickly; it's about ensuring your future solo journey offers options, not just survival—reflecting God's provision through faithful planting long before harvest arrives.

Faith-Based Principles of Stewardship

Stewardship begins when you translate conviction into concrete action. Biblical stewardship isn't passive gratitude—it's actively managing what God has entrusted to you. When the Israelites brought materials for the tabernacle in Exodus 35, they didn't compare their gifts to others. They contributed from their capacity. Your stewardship journey starts exactly where you are.

Conduct a possession audit this week. Walk through your home and document what you own: furniture, electronics, clothing, tools, books you've never opened. The average American household contains roughly 300,000 items. Most of us possess far more than we realize, and that abundance carries responsibility.

Ask two questions about each significant item: Am I using this? and Could this serve someone else better? When unused provision sits idle while others lack, we create spiritual imbalance. Choose one item this month to donate, sell, or lend. Releasing possessions often releases anxiety along with them.

Now examine how your money reflects your stated values. Print your bank statement from last month and highlight three categories: essentials, discretionary spending, and kingdom investment. Calculate the percentages. A 2018 Lifeway Research study revealed that 66% of Protestant churchgoers give away 10% or less of their income. This gap between priorities and allocation offers diagnostic insight into where your heart truly rests.

If kingdom investment falls below 5%, increase it by just 1% next month through automatic transfer to your church or a vetted ministry. Stewardship develops through consistent action, not isolated gestures.

Finally, identify one pending financial decision—a purchase, a work opportunity, a subscription to cancel. Pray over it using Proverbs 3:9: "Honor the Lord with your wealth, with the first fruits of all your crops." Does this choice honor God's ownership, or does fear drive it? Decide and act within seventy-two hours. Stewardship requires timely decisions; endless deliberation becomes its own form of disobedience.

Financial security built on faith isn't about achieving perfection—it's about making consistent, intentional choices that honor both your resources and your spiritual values. Once you've tracked your spending, established your baseline, and begun building emergency reserves, you're ready to transform these practices into enduring systems of faithful stewardship.

Start with automation. Set up automatic transfers on a specific day each month—perhaps the fifteenth, when your paycheck clears—to move funds into savings, retirement accounts, or giving. This simple act removes willpower from the equation. You're not deciding whether to save each month; you're honoring a commitment you've already made. Automation demonstrates active trust that God provides for today while preparing for tomorrow's unknowns.

Stewardship transforms from obligation to worship when you value the discipline itself. Remember the widow's two coins? Their significance lay not in their monetary value but in the trust they represented—given from poverty, yet given freely. Your $50 monthly investment or 1% increase in giving reflects the same principle. God values faithfulness over impressive totals.

Resistance will come. Your mind will generate compelling excuses: this month is different, skip the transfer, that subscription you know is wasteful suddenly feels essential. This isn't failure, it's the natural friction that accompanies meaningful change. The challenge isn't avoiding resistance; it's acting despite it.

Review your finances quarterly, not daily. Assess what's working, adjust what isn't, and notice recurring patterns. Some months will exceed your expectations; others will fall short. Financial stewardship isn't linear progress, it's consistent direction maintained through varied terrain. When unexpected expenses arrive, your emergency fund absorbs them without derailing your journey. During market fluctuations, your steady contributions allow you to buy low when others panic.

This foundation—tracking, protecting, investing, giving—creates clarity. It frees you to focus on what matters beyond mere survival, building capacity to respond to opportunity rather than merely react to crisis. True security doesn't originate in accumulated totals but in proven systems that function whether you're exhausted, inspired, or simply neutral.

These practices aren't endpoints. They're infrastructure supporting your broader journey, where financial stability becomes a platform for purpose, connection, and the specific calling God is preparing you to fulfill.

Chapter 8

Creating Meaningful Connections Without Losing Yourself

Understanding the Value of Meaningful Relationships

A woman rebuilds her entire identity in silence over fourteen months, learning to pray without borrowed language, budget without panic, and sit through evenings that stretch toward infinity. Then a coworker invites her to coffee.

She freezes.

The instinct, after months of hard-won self-sufficiency, is to protect what solitude has built. You've stopped needing constant validation, learned your own rhythms, discovered that God meets you reliably in the 6 a.m. stillness. Why risk diluting that clarity by letting someone else in?

But self-sufficiency was never meant to become isolation.

Neuroscience reveals what Scripture has always known: humans are wired for connection at the cellular level. Mirror neurons fire when we observe others' emotions, creating literal resonance between minds. Oxytocin released during meaningful conversation reduces cortisol and inflammation. The Harvard Study of Adult Development, tracking thousands over eighty years, proves that the quality—not quantity—of relationships predicts longevity more reliably than exercise, diet, or genetics combined.

This biological imperative finds its spiritual counterpart in community. Paul's writing about believers as members of one body describes functional reality, not poetic metaphor. Your gifts remain dormant until activated through service to others. Your blind spots stay invisible until someone who loves you names them.

Solitude teaches you who you are. Community reveals what you're for.

Meaningful connection means reciprocal vulnerability sustained over time—not casual exchanges, shared hobbies, or parallel presence. It's the difference between someone who knows what you do and someone who knows what you carry.

Five hundred Facebook friends cannot replace one person who notices when your smile stops reaching your eyes. A calendar packed with social obligations offers no guarantee against crushing loneliness. Research from the Journal of Social and Personal Relationships confirms that perceived social isolation—the quality gap between desired and actual intimacy—damages health more severely than objective measures of time spent alone. This distinction matters desperately because American culture conflates visibility with connection, measuring relational health through metrics designed for performance: invitations received, group chats maintained, networking events attended. But these superficial acquaintances—people who recognize your face, remember your job title, exchange pleasantries at church—function primarily as social scaffolding, providing the comforting illusion of belonging without requiring the discomfort of being known.

Depth, conversely, emerges through specific practices that most acquaintances never approach: naming fear without needing it fixed, confessing failure without performing repentance, asking for help without apologizing for the imposition. It requires showing up when nothing's wrong and staying present when everything is.

This reciprocal vulnerability builds slowly through accumulated small exchanges that prove safety—then one crisis reveals you've been building infrastructure all along.

For those navigating solitude, this distinction becomes critical. You don't need more people. You need the right people—two or three relationships where masks can drop, where your becoming doesn't threaten their comfort, where silence doesn't require filling.

That kind of connection doesn't dilute what you've built alone. It completes it.

The work you've done in solitude has been sacred—discovering who you are when no one's watching, building strength in the quiet presence of God, learning to stand alone without falling apart. This foundation isn't something to abandon as you reach toward connection. It's the very thing that makes authentic relationship possible.

Without this groundwork, you'd enter relationships the way most people do: searching for someone to complete you, to fill the void, to make you feel whole. But you've already found wholeness in God's presence. You've already discovered that your worth isn't determined by another person's attention or affection. This changes everything about how you connect.

Authentic connection doesn't require you to diminish yourself, to make yourself smaller so someone else feels comfortable, to abandon the boundaries you've carefully established. It asks something different: that you show up fully as yourself while creating space for someone else to do the same.

This means learning to be with people without losing yourself in them. It means maintaining the spiritual practices that sustained you through isolation even when your calendar fills with social obligations. It means saying no when you need solitude to recharge, without apology or elaborate explanation.

Start small. Choose one person you trust and practice showing them something true about yourself—a struggle, a hope, a fear you haven't voiced aloud. Notice what happens when you let someone witness your authentic self without trying to manage their response.

Then notice what happens when you witness theirs.

Setting Boundaries to Protect Your Solo Strength

Boundaries aren't walls erected to isolate you from the world. They're the sacred space where you end and another person begins—the invisible line that honors both connection and selfhood.

After months of solitude, you've developed an instinct for what nourishes versus what depletes. Coffee with Sarah leaves you energized and inspired. Dinner with your sister requires three days of recovery. A conversation with Mark feels balanced, reciprocal. Your cousin's endless venting leaves you spiritually hollow, emotionally spent.

Personal boundaries define what you will and won't accept in relationships based on your actual capacity, not theoretical generosity or obligatory sacrifice. They answer questions most people never dare articulate: How much emotional labor can I provide before resentment poisons the well? How many social obligations can I sustain while protecting sacred prayer time? Which topics am I willing to discuss, and which remain between me and God? When do I need to leave, regardless of social pressure or guilt?

Without clear boundaries, every relationship becomes a negotiation you're destined to lose.

You say yes when your soul screams no. You stay when every fiber begs to leave. You absorb someone else's chaos because declining feels selfish, even cruel. Then resentment builds—not toward them, but toward yourself for violating limits you never had the courage to voice.

Boundaries require self-knowledge first—the intimate awareness that solitude provides. You've discovered you need Tuesday mornings alone, that certain conversations trigger unhealed wounds, that you cannot rescue others without abandoning your own stability. This isn't selfishness. This is stewardship of the life God entrusted to you.

Rachel had watched her mother become invisible.

For thirty years, her mother said yes to every request, absorbed every criticism, and apologized for needs she never voiced. When she finally collapsed from exhaustion at fifty-eight, the same people who'd depleted her acted surprised. Rachel decided differently. After her divorce, she began stating limits aloud: "I can't host Christmas this year." "I need to leave by eight." "That topic isn't something I'm willing to discuss." The pushback was immediate—her sister called her selfish, her father suggested she was "building walls," and friends who'd grown accustomed to her endless availability interpreted boundaries as rejection.

Yet some individuals responded with grace. Sarah didn't guilt-trip when Rachel declined last-minute invitations. Mark adjusted conversation when she named a painful subject. Her pastor honored her request for email communication instead of surprise visits. These were the relationships Rachel found worth cultivating.

Others escalated. Her cousin showed up unannounced "because we're family." Her college roommate persisted with intrusive questions after being asked to stop. One former friend responded to Rachel's gentle I'm not available that evening with a forty-minute lecture about Christian duty and sacrificial love.

Boundaries reveal who truly values you. Individuals who have benefited from a lack of boundaries often escalate tactics when limits are introduced—employing guilt, manipulation, or relational pressure to restore the previous imbalance. Conversely, those who genuinely respect boundaries demonstrate higher empathy and relational reciprocity, prioritizing mutual respect over convenience. Boundaries do not alienate those who genuinely value you; they expose those who exploit silence, creating space for relationships built on mutual honor rather than continuous depletion.

Some friendships appear supportive until you examine what they actually offer. These often fall into two types: cheerleaders and witnesses. Cheerleaders encourage from a distance, offering enthusiastic affirmation that requires nothing of them—they text "You're amazing!" but vanish when you need someone to sit with you through the hard middle of grief. They celebrate your victories but grow uncomfortable with your doubts. Their support is real but fundamentally shallow, collapsing under the weight of sustained need.

Witnesses show up differently. They ask uncomfortable questions because they care about your actual wellbeing, not your performance of it. They notice when you're lying to yourself. They remember what you said three weeks ago and follow up. When you're spiraling, they don't rush to fix it—they stay present while you find your footing. This kind of friendship costs them something: time, emotional energy, the discomfort of watching someone struggle without intervening prematurely.

But even genuine witnesses have limitations you must respect. Your college friend who walked with you through the divorce may not have capacity for your current financial crisis—her father just died, her bandwidth is gone. The mentor who offered profound spiritual guidance might be terrible with practical advice about career transitions. Expecting any single person to meet all relational needs isn't intimacy; it's exploitation disguised as closeness.

Watch what fails under pressure. When you're genuinely struggling—not performing struggle for sympathy, but actually unraveling—who remains? Whose presence doesn't require you to minimize your pain or rush your healing? That person, even if it's only one, matters more than a dozen surface-level connections that evaporate when tested.

Some relationships were only meant to carry you through one season. And that's not failure—it's God's design.

Maintaining boundaries begins with one unglamorous practice: deciding in advance. Before the phone rings, before the guilt arrives, before someone's disappointment makes you question what you know is true—decide what you will and won't do. Write it down. Sunday evenings are for solitude and prayer, non-negotiable. You don't accept last-minute requests that disrupt established rhythms. You don't explain your no three different ways hoping someone will finally approve.

When someone pushes—and they will—have one simple sentence ready. "That doesn't work for me" requires no justification. Notice the instinct to soften it, to apologize, to provide elaborate reasons that invite negotiation. Resist that instinct.

Track what depletes you versus what replenishes. After each significant interaction, spend two minutes noting: Did this leave me more or less able to show up as myself? Did I feel pressure to perform, minimize, or manage someone else's emotions? Over three weeks, patterns emerge with startling clarity. The acquaintance who vents endlessly leaves you mentally exhausted. The friend who never reciprocates your listening ear acts as a drain on your emotional resources, like withdrawing from an account with no deposits.

Some relationships require renegotiation, not elimination. Tell your sister: "I can't do daily phone calls, but let's talk Thursdays at seven." Give your small group leader: "I need to step back for this season—I'll return when I have capacity." People who respect you will adjust. People who need you diminished will protest that you're being selfish, difficult, cold.

Their discomfort is not your emergency.

Your wholeness is not up for negotiation.

Engaging Authentically with Community

Finding communities that align with your values requires intentionality, not passive waiting. Most people drift into groups by proximity or obligation—the church closest to home, the small group their neighbor invited them to—then wonder why these spaces feel hollow. You've done sacred work in solitude. Now use what you discovered there as your compass.

Begin with what you actually believe, not what you think you should believe. Review your journal from the last three months. Which values surface repeatedly? Which biblical principles anchored you when everything else felt uncertain? Maybe it's radical honesty about struggle, maybe it's contemplative worship over performance-driven praise, maybe it's service to the marginalized. Identify three non-negotiables—convictions so core that compromising them makes you feel fraudulent. These become your criteria for spaces where your faith can flourish authentically.

Research before committing your precious time and energy. Visit a church's website: do they acknowledge real suffering or only celebrate victories? Examine a volunteer organization's actual work, not just their polished mission statement. Attend one gathering as an observer, paying attention to the margins—how do people treat newcomers? Do conversations venture beneath pleasant surfaces? Does someone's visible struggle make the room tense?

You're not searching for perfect people. You're discerning whether this specific community creates space for who you actually are.

Test alignment through small experiments rather than premature commitments. Attend three sessions before deciding anything. Volunteer for one project, not the entire leadership team. Have coffee with someone whose presence felt genuine. Notice how your body responds: Do you leave energized or needing days to recover? Can you voice honest doubt without feeling pressure to reassure everyone you're still faithful? Does this group's expression of faith resonate with what you discovered in solitude, or does it require you to become smaller?

Some communities won't fit, and that's wisdom, not failure. Walk away without guilt. Alignment isn't about finding flawless people—it's about discovering spaces where your journey toward wholeness is honored, not corrected.

Protecting what you've built in solitude requires discerning engagement with community, not withdrawal. In quiet moments, you've learned to hear God's voice, ceased performing for validation, and discovered your true self unobserved. This inner sanctuary is sacred.

Do not relinquish it the moment community provides comfort.

Boundaries provide the essential framework for authentic relationships, rather than betraying connection. Declining to host another draining event affirms the solitude vital for your wholeness. Leaving a gathering at eight instead of midnight honors the rhythm sustaining your spiritual life. While some may interpret your limits as rejection, their discomfort is not your responsibility. Healthy boundaries aren't barriers—they're invitations to genuine connection. They tell others: This is who I am. This is what I can offer. This is where I meet God.

Communities worth joining celebrate the self-knowledge solitude reveals, instead of demanding its abandonment. Observe responses when you voice a boundary. Respectful individuals adjust without guilt-tripping you. Others, accustomed to your limitless giving, will call you selfish, lecture you on duty, or escalate demands.

Their reaction clarifies everything: Boundaries expose whether someone values you or merely requires your diminishment.

Regularly reassess your capacity, as it constantly shifts. The friend group that energized you last month might drain you this week. A meaningful volunteer commitment can become an obligation when your reserves are low. After each interaction, ask yourself: Did this nourish or deplete me? Can I articulate my needs, or am I reverting to performance? Your solitude journal already trained you to recognize these patterns. Continue consulting it. Listen to that inner voice you've worked so hard to uncover.

Community's role is to enhance spiritual growth, not to replace it. Fiercely protect the morning prayer practice you cultivated alone. Uphold the boundaries you established, even as relationships deepen. Allow your self-knowledge to guide every connection. The wholeness you discovered in solitude becomes your greatest gift to others—not your sacrifice to them.

Your discoveries about yourself, God, and your genuine needs establish a permanent foundation. Build every relationship upon this understanding. This integration creates a unique synergy, one neither solitude nor community can achieve independently: a life where deep connection never compromises your identity, and personal space never implies isolation. This is Faithful Independence in action—rooted in God, extending toward others, never losing yourself in the process.

Chapter 9

Creating Routines and Structure for Your Solo Days

Designing Your Daily Framework for Wellness

Your first conscious moments each morning hold extraordinary power. The cortisol awakening response naturally floods your system with stress hormones within minutes of waking, and what you do in that window shapes everything that follows. Those who immediately grab their phones, scrolling through news or email, amplify this physiological stress response, launching their day from a place of reaction rather than intention. But those who claim these minutes for something deliberate—prayer, reflection, conscious breathing and some stretching and soft movements. Being grateful to God for another day—report significantly lower anxiety and a profound sense of agency that carries through their entire day.

Your morning doesn't need elaborate rituals borrowed from productivity gurus.

It needs intention. When you live alone, no external structure creates natural rhythm. No spouse's schedule. No children's needs imposing non-negotiable anchors. This freedom becomes treacherous when you drift into each morning without purpose, allowing circumstances to dictate your internal state before you've even decided who you are today. The world floods in—notifications, obligations, yesterday's regrets, tomorrow's anxieties—rushing past the threshold before you've established your foundation.

0

Physical movement changes your brain chemistry in ways that prayer alone cannot.

A thirty-minute brisk walk triggers the release of endorphins and brain-derived neurotrophic factors, chemicals that strengthen neural pathways and counteract the damage of chronic stress. Your body holds grief that words cannot reach, storing trauma in tight shoulders, shallow breathing, and relentless tension. Movement releases what rumination only reinforces. You don't need athleticism or specialized equipment—you need consistency. The same walk, the same time, three mornings each week, until your body anticipates this rhythm and the conscious choice becomes ingrained habit.

But movement without rest becomes another form of running away.

Intentional rest—true restorative pause, not distraction or collapse—might be the hardest discipline for those living alone. No one notices if you work until midnight, skip meals, or wear exhaustion like armor for three straight days. Rest requires valuing your own humanity enough to stop before something forces you to stop, trusting that the world continues without your constant effort.

Balancing body and mind means refusing the false choice between physical health and spiritual depth. These aren't competing priorities. They're interwoven realities, each creating capacity for the other, each compromised when the other is neglected.

Building a daily schedule matters because structure becomes the external scaffolding that holds you upright when internal motivation fails. When you live alone, no one notices if you sleep until noon, skip breakfast, or spend four hours scrolling through your phone. The absence of accountability isn't freedom—it's a vacuum where discipline collapses under the weight of grief, fear, or simple inertia.

Your body craves predictable rhythms. When wake times fluctuate wildly, when meals happen randomly, when bedtime becomes whenever exhaustion forces surrender, your circadian system destabilizes. Sleep quality deteriorates, appetite regulation fails, and emotional resilience crumbles. Extensive research in chronobiology confirms what your exhausted body already knows: individuals with inconsistent daily routines often report significantly higher levels of cortisol and inflammatory markers, physiological signatures of chronic stress and depression.

But rigid schedules can become another form of control masquerading as health.

The true objective is sustainability, not perfection. An inflexible routine—one where a disrupted morning triggers shame and total abandonment—is not structure; it's fragility disguised as discipline. You need enough framework to prevent chaos, enough flexibility to honor your humanity. A single mother working unpredictable shifts requires a different architecture than a retiree structuring wide-open days, yet both benefit from deliberate rhythms anchoring their weeks.

Without this balance, two patterns emerge with brutal predictability: either punishing rigidity that collapses at the first disruption, or complete formlessness where days blur into weeks with nothing to mark their passing. Both leave you depleted, convinced that you're failing at something others manage effortlessly. God's design for your solo days isn't chains or chaos—it's compassionate consistency that allows you to thrive.

Incorporating Purposeful Activities into Your Routine

Purposeful activities occupy solitude differently than distractions disguised as productivity. When you alphabetize your spice rack for the third time this month, you're avoiding something. When you spend two hours learning basic carpentry to repair that wobbly chair, you're engaging capability. The distinction lies in intentionality—purposeful work addresses genuine needs or expresses authentic values, while distractions merely consume time until you feel justified in stopping.

This matters profoundly in solitude because meaningful activity generates internal evidence of growth that no external validation can provide. You're not performing for anyone's approval or meeting someone else's expectations. The woman who teaches herself basic plumbing doesn't do it because her friends will be impressed—she does it because competence builds dignity, and dignity erodes when you feel helpless in your own space. Each completed task becomes tangible proof that aloneness doesn't equal stagnation. You are becoming, not simply waiting.

The content of purposeful activities varies wildly depending on your circumstances and temperament. One person finds meaning in morning gardening, another in volunteer tax preparation for elderly neighbors. What matters isn't the specific activity but whether it addresses three essential questions: Does this require something from me beyond passive consumption? Does this align with values I've actually chosen, not inherited? Will I have concrete evidence when it's finished?

Activities lacking these elements may feel productive but leave you oddly empty afterward.

Real passion reveals itself not through applause, but through the quiet persistence you maintain when no one's watching.

Discovering what truly resonates requires experimentation without the tyranny of immediate mastery. Living alone grants you sacred privacy for honest exploration—no one witnesses your off-key guitar practice or your awkward first watercolor attempts. This solitude becomes permission to fail spectacularly, to abandon pursuits that sounded appealing but feel hollow, to stumble toward activities that energize you even when they're difficult. The freedom to explore without an audience is itself a gift, transforming your alone time into a laboratory for self-discovery.

Start with exposure, not commitment. Attend one pottery class. Borrow bread-making equipment before investing in your own. Volunteer for a single trail maintenance day. Notice what occupies your mind during the activity and what lingers afterward. Genuine passion creates a specific internal signature: time distorts, self-consciousness fades, and you experience complete absorption where effort feels effortless.

But this flow alone isn't sufficient evidence of true calling.

The deeper question asks whether this activity connects to something beyond yourself. Does it express gratitude for creation? Does it develop capacities that could become instruments of purpose? A hobby that merely distracts differs fundamentally from a passion that aligns with God's design for your unique gifts. The carpentry you practice in solitude might eventually build wheelchair ramps. The photography you pursue alone might document stories that otherwise go unwitnessed.

Passion discovered in private creates capacity for contribution you cannot yet imagine.

Translation from discovery to daily practice requires specific time architecture, not vague intentions. You cannot rely on finding time—alone, you will always find reasons to postpone. Instead, assign your purposeful activity to a precise recurring slot: Tuesday and Thursday evenings at seven, Saturday mornings before errands, Sunday afternoons when the week's obligations have lifted. Calendar it as non-negotiable, treating this commitment to yourself with the same respect you'd extend to a doctor's appointment or work meeting.

But schedules fail when they ignore energy patterns.

Morning people who force creative work into late evenings create resistance, not rhythm. Notice when your body and mind naturally feel most receptive—some experience clarity in early morning silence, while others find their thoughts sharpen after dark. Your routine must accommodate your actual physiology, not an idealized version of who you think you should be. God designed you with specific capacities that fluctuate predictably throughout each day, and honoring this design is stewardship, not self-indulgence.

This approach falters most commonly around week four, when novelty evaporates and repetition feels suffocating. You'll encounter the brutal truth that consistency precedes inspiration, not the reverse. The commitment to the scheduled slot arrives whether you feel motivated or not. This is precisely where solitude becomes either crucible or escape hatch. Without external accountability, you must decide whether this activity genuinely matters or merely sounded appealing when life felt emptier.

The litmus test asks whether you return after missing a session.

Missing once is inevitable; missing three times consecutively reveals the activity hasn't earned its place in your life. Release it without shame and redirect that time toward something that survives contact with reality. When routines do take root, protect them ferociously. Your alone time makes these commitments vulnerable to every external request, every spontaneous invitation. Saying no to others so you can say yes to purposeful solitude isn't selfish—it's recognizing that the person you're becoming in private will determine what you can offer when community eventually arrives.

Once your personal routine is established, seeking connection becomes a natural next step. Select one purposeful activity—painting, hiking, woodworking, or a book club—and intentionally share it with others. Seek out local art workshops with weekly open sessions, hiking associations organizing weekend treks, or craftsmanship guilds where artisans exchange tools and techniques. While online forums can introduce you, genuine connection thrives in shared physical presence, offering a depth digital interaction cannot replicate.

Attend three times before deciding whether the group fits.

The first session will likely feel awkward, the second slightly less so. By the third, you'll discern whether these people energize or deplete you, whether the activity deepens or diminishes in their company. Not every group deserves your continued presence. Some communities cultivate competition rather than encouragement, mistaking constant socializing for genuine connection. Trust your instincts when something feels misaligned.

When you find authentic resonance, contribute before you consume. Arrive early to help arrange chairs. Offer to coordinate the group's calendar. Share materials you've accumulated. These small acts signal investment beyond simply extracting value, and groups remember who shows up reliably. Reliability, not charm, builds trust within a group. Your self-sufficiency, honed in solitude, now allows you to contribute without needing external validation. People notice when you choose their company for its own sake, not out of desperation—a stance that cultivates genuine mutual respect. Over months, acquaintances become colleagues, then friends, not through forced intimacy but through returning to the same work alongside the same people, discovering gradually that shared purpose fosters connection distinct from what solitary work offers.

Building Momentum: Staying Committed to Your Structure

Start with one quantifiable goal attached to your routine. Not sweeping transformation, nor profound personal reinvention. Pick something measurable: meditate for seven minutes three mornings this week, cook dinner at home four times, or complete two chapters in that book on your nightstand. Write the goal on paper and assign it a visible deadline—this week only.

Seven days. Sunday to Sunday.

After the week ends, record what actually happened. Three meditation sessions completed equals three. No rounding up. No credit for good intentions. Just facts. Progress doesn't announce itself through sudden euphoria or radical life changes. It accumulates in quiet increments so modest you'll dismiss them if you're not deliberately watching. Completing those meditation sessions might not cure your loneliness, but it does prove you're capable of keeping promises to yourself when no one else would notice either way. That evidence matters more than the meditation itself. You're building the infrastructure of self-trust, and self-trust cannot be constructed through abstract affirmations—only through documented follow-through.

Celebration feels uncomfortable for many living alone because who celebrates with an audience of one? You do. Deliberately. When you hit a weekly goal, mark it physically: cross it off a visible list, move a token from one jar to another, or text a friend the specific outcome. These physical actions serve as cognitive anchors, registering accomplishment directly in your nervous system.

Your brain needs tangible proof that effort yields results, especially when you're spending most hours in your own company without external recognition. The celebration doesn't need to be elaborate—it needs to happen. For goals that stretch beyond a single week, break them into seven-day fragments with distinct checkpoints. Learning conversational Spanish becomes: complete three lessons this week. Building stamina becomes: walk fifteen minutes four times. The marker moves every Sunday. You either met the threshold or you didn't.

When you don't, adjust the goal downward rather than abandoning it. Four times was ambitious? Try three next week. The commitment is to continuation with honest recalibration, not to flawless execution that collapses at the first disruption. Track three months this way and patterns emerge that reveal what's sustainable versus what sounded good in theory.

You've built something most people never attempt: structure that exists whether anyone else notices. Yet here's the truth—structure alone won't sustain you when motivation vanishes at six in the morning on a cold

Tuesday. Accountability partners, journaling systems, and faith-based support groups provide the crucial load-bearing framework that transforms private commitment into sustainable practice, holding your resolve in place when willpower falters.

Community, even in solitude, isn't contradiction. It's wisdom.

The accountability partner who checks in Friday mornings, the journal that captures three weeks of consistent meditation sessions followed by four days of nothing, the support group that meets Thursday evenings and notices when you're absent—each creates a feedback loop stronger than willpower alone. Witnessed commitment carries different weight than private intention. When someone else knows you planned to pray each morning this week, missing Thursday doesn't just disappoint you—it becomes data you'll discuss, a gap that demands honest examination rather than convenient amnesia. Research consistently shows that public commitment significantly increases follow-through, leveraging both social connection and our deep desire for consistency.

Journaling reveals patterns invisible in the moment. Flipping back through two months of entries, you'll notice that disruptions cluster around specific triggers: Sunday evenings, the week before your ex picks up the kids, anniversaries you thought you'd forgotten. That awareness transforms reactive collapse into strategic preparation. Next time that date approaches, you'll schedule extra support, lower your expectations, and protect your routine with deliberate reinforcement rather than discovering—again—that willpower fails under predictable stress.

Faith-based groups offer something distinct: theological permission to struggle without shame.

When your journal records another week of inconsistent prayer and mounting frustration, the group reminds you that spiritual formation happens through failure and return, not flawless consistency. God meets you in the gaps, not just the victories. The routines you've built—held by accountability, tracked through journaling, supported by community—teach you how to construct a life that holds its shape under pressure, how to return after disruption, how to trust yourself even when you're the only one watching. That capacity transfers. The discipline required to maintain Thursday evening commitments when Netflix beckons is identical to the discipline required for financial stability, career transitions, and eventually—when the time comes—entering new relationships from wholeness rather than need.

You're cultivating the ability to keep promises to yourself, even without external scrutiny.

Chapter 10

Remaining Open to Future Relationships Without Losing Your Peace

Understanding Healthy Openness vs. Desperate Longing

Research in attachment theory reveals something profound about independence. Some people display what psychologists call defensive independence—a brittle self-sufficiency that masks deep fear and registers as physiological stress in their bodies. Others demonstrate secure autonomy, characterized by lower anxiety and richer connections with others.

Outwardly, these two groups look remarkably similar. Internally, they're living opposite realities.

Defensive independence operates from scarcity, building walls against pain by preemptively rejecting possibility. This mindset views vulnerability as devastation, making permanent fortification seem like the only logical solution. It whispers, why risk the good life I've built alone?

Healthy openness works differently. It neither seeks completion through others nor rigidly bolts every door. Instead, it rests in the peace of solitude's discoveries—identity anchored, rhythms established, purpose clarified—while remaining genuinely available for relationships that lead to mutual flourishing. This openness trusts divine timing, distinguishing between lonely desperation that accepts anyone and discerning availability that welcomes the right someone.

You've already proven you don't need another person to complete your life.

The real challenge now? Maintaining that hard-won wholeness while remaining genuinely open to shared life, should God's timing align.

Desperate longing wears many masks, but its presence becomes unmistakable once you learn its language.

You find yourself engineering encounters—choosing the coffee shop where you might run into someone interesting, accepting invitations to events you'd normally decline, scrolling through profiles with the same restless energy that once masked deeper pain. Your internal narrative shifts from I'm content to I'm still alone, a subtle rewording that transforms peace into problem. Strangers become potential partners before they've spoken a word, and you construct entire futures from a passing smile.

The physical signs emerge too. That hollow aches when friends mention their partners. Silence that once felt restorative now feels accusatory. Saturday evenings—your sacred solitude—suddenly stretch unbearably long.

Your carefully built rhythms begin crumbling. Prayer becomes petition. Journaling circles the same questions about timing and worthiness. Creative projects gather dust because they require the settled mind you no longer possess.

Most telling? You notice yourself compromising non-negotiable boundaries, entertaining attention from people whose values contradict yours, justifying clear warning signs as nobody's perfect.

Unhealthy attachment to the idea of relationship actively sabotages the self-discovery you've worked to cultivate, replacing God's peace with restless striving.

Recognizing desperate longing is one thing. Cultivating healthy openness requires building something entirely different—a posture that welcomes possibility without grasping at it.

Begin with ruthless honesty about your current state. Before entertaining the possibility of relationship, ask yourself these questions: Does your personal worth still rely on external validation, or is God's valuation genuinely sufficient? Can you envision a fulfilling year ahead with no romantic prospect? Is remaining single preferable to compromising the boundaries you've established? If defensiveness rises instead of calm clarity, you're not ready yet.

Healthy openness means protecting the infrastructure you've built. Your prayer rhythms, creative pursuits, community connections, financial disciplines—these aren't negotiable. Notice attraction without assigning it cosmic significance. Feel hope without manufacturing destiny.

Embrace environments where meaningful connection occurs organically. Serve alongside others. Pursuing genuine interests. Invest in friendships without agenda. The strongest relationships emerge from shared purpose and values, not engineered romance. When God's timing aligns with your wholeness, connection unfolds naturally.

Ultimately, healthy openness requires placing hope in God's faithfulness, not in a relationship outcome. Cultivate gratitude for your present life—the peace forged through solitude; the self-knowledge earned through honest wrestling. Approach future possibilities with quiet expectation, not anxious anticipation.

When the right person appears, you'll recognize them not by intensity but by how their presence enhances rather than disrupts your wholeness.

Cultivating Inner Peace While Anticipating Future Relationships

Inner peace isn't the absence of desire—it's the steady ground beneath your feet that doesn't shift when desire arrives.

When someone attractive enters your life, genuine peace allows you to notice the pull without spiraling. Your pulse quickens, conversation flows easily, and you wonder if this might be something. But you don't manufacture reasons to text them at midnight. You don't scroll their social profiles constructing narratives from breadcrumbs. You don't cancel Thursday plans with friends because they might possibly be available. Peace reveals itself through non-reactivity, that hallmark of secure attachment where you approach new connections from a place of inner stability, enjoying initial interactions without spiraling into future projections or seeking external validation.

Without this center, relationship readiness becomes performance.

You present a curated version of yourself, terrified that authentic you—with your mortgage anxiety, your Wednesday pottery class, your need for alone time—will drive them away. You abandon morning prayer because they texted. You cancel the boundary-setting conversation because conflict might end things. This is desperation masquerading as openness.

True readiness means the life you've built doesn't crumble when someone enters it. Your budget holds. Your friendships remain. Your non-negotiables stay non-negotiable. The person who fits will enhance this structure, not demand its demolition. Peace fosters a mindset that is selective rather than desperate, patient rather than grasping. Instead of "please choose me," your underlying question becomes are we genuinely compatible?

Sarah built her evenings around noise. After eighteen months alone following her husband's death, she scheduled back-to-back activities—Zumba Mondays, book club Tuesdays, volunteer shifts Wednesdays—until the calendar resembled a defensive perimeter. When her counselor suggested twenty minutes of daily mindfulness practice, Sarah laughed. "Sit with my thoughts? That's when the panic starts."

Yet research consistently shows that structured mindfulness practice reshapes both mind and body. A 2013 study in Health Psychology found participants engaging in mindfulness-based stress reduction showed measurably lower cortisol levels and reduced anxiety compared to control groups. The mechanism wasn't mystical mindfulness creates cognitive distance between stimulus and response, building the neurological pause that transforms "someone smiled at me" from cosmic sign into simple pleasant moment.

Sarah started with guided meditation apps during her morning coffee. Nothing elaborate.

Within six weeks, something shifted. An attractive colleague invited her to lunch, and instead of the familiar spiral—texting friends for analysis, checking his ring finger seventeen times, imagining their hypothetical future—she simply enjoyed the conversation. The attraction registered without hijacking her afternoon. She didn't construct narratives or engineer follow-up encounters. This was non-reactivity, the fruit of practicing observation without immediate interpretation, allowing feelings to exist without controlling her.

Self-care operates similarly as unglamorous discipline. Maintaining your Thursday therapy appointments even when dating begins. Guarding your morning routine. Keeping the budget that survived the separation intact. These sustained practices offer far more than bubble baths and face masks—they establish the foundation for your emotional and financial stability, ensuring you remain whole whether someone stays or leaves.

Not every fear deserves equal weight. Discernment distinguishes between protective caution and paralyzing anxiety—one rooted in lived experience, the other in catastrophic projection that hasn't happened yet.

Consider someone recently independent after a difficult divorce who feels drawn to another person at a community service project. Two fears emerge simultaneously: fear of repeating patterns from their failed marriage, and fear that any romantic interest signals weakness after years of hard-won independence. Only one fear deserves their attention. The first arises from concrete history—an ex-spouse's destructive habits, a tendency to rationalize red flags, the financial wreckage they've spent years repairing. The second is simply shame dressed as discernment, the internalized voice insisting that wholeness means permanent solitude.

They needed to honor the first fear by establishing non-negotiable boundaries around specific behaviors and transparency. The second fear required acknowledgment, then release.

Even legitimate caution fails when applied rigidly. Some people raised in chaotic homes develop such sensitive threat detection that green flags register as suspicious kindness feels manipulative, consistency seems too good to be true, healthy conflict resolution triggers waiting for inevitable explosion. When perception, shaped by past wounds, cannot distinguish between genuine concern and trauma-fueled hypervigilance, trusted community becomes essential.

A therapist, spiritual director, or brutally honest friend offers external perspective when your internal compass spins wildly. They notice when you're protecting yourself wisely—and when you're simply protecting your fear.

Begin with a clear-eyed assessment of where you stand right now. Create three distinct lists: your non-negotiable boundaries, born from painful lessons you refuse to relive; the infrastructure of peace you've carefully constructed—prayer rhythms, creative commitments, cherished friendships, financial disciplines; and the specific fears that surface when you imagine future connection. Don't analyze or judge. Simply document what exists.

Guard that second list as carefully as you honor the first.

When interest in someone new emerges, ask yourself one clarifying question: Does this person's presence enhance or disrupt the foundation you've built? Enhancement appears as genuine celebration of your Tuesday morning prayer time, thoughtful questions about your creative work, and respect for established friendships. Disruption arrives more quietly with gentle suggestions to skip accountability group "just this once," questioning why you require solitude, creating urgency that destabilizes your carefully cultivated rhythm. Notice the difference.

Practice observing attraction without assigning it cosmic significance. Someone intrigues you at a volunteer shift or church gathering. Rather than mentally planning your shared future or dismissing the feeling entirely, simply acknowledge I notice I'm drawn to this person. Then return to the present moment. This disciplines your heart to experience interest without obsession or flight, building the muscle of balanced openness.

Building a Fulfilling Life In The Here and Now

Gratitude requires infrastructure. Most people approach appreciation like rainfall—waiting for it to arrive spontaneously, hoping circumstances trigger warmth. But sustainable gratitude functions like irrigation: deliberate channels built to reach roots even during drought.

Start with the gratitude inventory. Every evening for fourteen consecutive days, write three specifics from that day. Not abstractions like "my health" but concrete details: a neighbor holding the door, the morning light through windows, your car starting in freezing temperatures. Notice the resistance around day four when this feel manufactured or silly. That resistance matters. Your brain, shaped by loss, has become hypervigilant to threaten survival mechanism that kept ancestors alive but now scans relentlessly for what's missing. Deliberately naming good rewires neural pathways, creating competing tracks that expand your vision beyond survival mode.

Beyond private journaling, gratitude becomes tangible through expressed acknowledgment. Once weekly, tell one specific person why their presence matters, using concrete details rather than generic praise.

Text your sister: "You check in every Tuesday without me asking means I don't carry everything alone." Email your therapist: "Your question last month about what I actually want, not what I should want, unlocked something." Write physical notes to service workers. This strengthens relational bonds and trains you to notice contribution in places you previously overlooked.

The most difficult gratitude targets what you didn't choose—your empty house, single income, unshared meals. This involves acknowledging specific growth that happened only because you walked through fire, without requiring pretense that loss feels good. Name one thing your solitude taught you that partnership would have obscured: the prayer depth, financial competence, or capacity for self-solace you discovered when no one else could carry the weight.

Passionate pursuits don't rescue you from aloneness—they reveal who you are when no one's watching.

This revelation matters more than distraction ever could. When you commit to woodworking, language learning, trail running, or volunteer work during solitary seasons, you're not filling time until something better arrives. You're building capacity through activities that function as laboratories for self-discovery. A pottery class teaches patience through failed vessels. Community garden work builds collaboration skills. A photography hobby trains your attention to notice beauty in ordinary moments. These aren't temporary placeholders—they're essential infrastructure for a thriving life, with or without partnership.

The peace you've cultivated isn't the absence of wanting. It's the stable ground beneath changing desires.

Through unglamorous repetition, you've established lasting foundations: prayer schedules that persist beyond inspiration, financial systems protecting against catastrophe, gratitude practices rewiring your attention from threat to presence. Integration means carrying forward what you've learned, not abandoning it when circumstances shift. The person who eventually fits your life will enhance what you've built, not require its demolition. They'll celebrate your Tuesday pottery sessions, not demand you sacrifice them. They'll respect your morning prayer rhythm rather than viewing it as time stolen from them.

This season has cultivated something profound—a life shaped deliberately rather than reactively. You've shifted from asking "How do

I endure this?" to "What becomes possible here?" That perspective change impacts everything. The practices sustaining you now build capacity for richer relationships later, creating tangible evidence that growth continues regardless of relationship status.

Chapter 11

Discovering Your Purpose and Living It Out Alone

Identifying Your Unique God-Given Calling

An individual in Pennsylvania discovered a profound sense of purpose while anonymously paying off $2,500 in school lunch debt at a local elementary school in 2023. This quiet act, performed without fanfare, sparked a certainty that felt like recognition, not revelation.

Your purpose isn't hiding in grand theology or waiting for dramatic confirmation. It's already present in the activities that make you forget to check your phone, the moments when hours vanish because you're so completely absorbed that time loses meaning.

Most believers approach calling backwards. They wait for divine skywriting, expecting God to interrupt ordinary life with extraordinary directives. But Scripture reveals a different pattern: Moses discovered his leadership capacity while defending the vulnerable, David's kingship emerged from faithful shepherding, and Esther's courage activated in crisis, not beforehand. Your unique calling lives in the intersection of three concrete realities: what engages you so completely that hours vanish, what specific needs you notice that others overlook, and what you do consistently when no external reward exists.

Not what impresses. Not what you think should matter. But what actually, persistently pulls your attention.

Track this week without analysis: Which conversations energize you? What problems do you solve unasked? When do you lose yourself completely? These questions aren't abstract exercises—they're invitations to recognize the divine fingerprints already marking your daily life, revealing the unique contributions only you can make to the world.

Prayer and meditation become your compass when purpose feels distant. This isn't about mystical experiences or perfect spiritual technique—it's structured conversation with the One who designed your journey from the beginning.

Honest prayer matters more than eloquent prayer. God doesn't require polished theology or carefully constructed petitions. Bring your raw questions, your frustration, your desperate need for direction. Many discover their calling during sleepless nights, processing loss and demanding answers: "What do I do with this pain? What purpose could this possibly serve?" These aren't irreverent questions—they're the beginning of genuine dialogue. Over time, those desperate demands transform into conversations, and answers emerge not as audible voices but as persistent, undeniable knowing.

Contemplative stillness creates space for divine response.

Set aside seven minutes. Sit without agenda or expectation. When thoughts intrude—and they will—gently return your attention to breath or a simple phrase: "Show me." This practice trains your attention away from mental noise toward subtle, underlying clarity. Answers rarely arrive as dramatic pronouncements. Instead, certain possibilities feel weighted differently. One path generates quiet resonance while others, however logical, feel hollow.

Divine guidance confirms itself through patterns: Scripture passages addressing your exact question, unsolicited conversations echoing emerging convictions, circumstances aligning without your manipulation. One confirmation proves nothing; three unrelated confirmations pointing the same direction demand attention. Sometimes clarity arrives as persistent discomfort with your current direction rather than enthusiasm for alternatives. Trust that, too.

Identifying your calling changes nothing if it stays locked inside your head.

The gap between spiritual conviction and tangible action is where most purpose dies—not through active rejection, but through passive waiting for perfect conditions that never arrive. Purpose manifests through ordinary decisions made Tuesday morning. You sense God calling you toward creative expression, community care, or meaningful work. The question isn't whether this conviction feels certain enough—it's what you'll do about it in the next seventy-two hours. Research one local nonprofit needing volunteers. Email one person already doing work that resonates. Spend thirty uninterrupted minutes on that project your hands have been itching to start.

Most people never act because they're terrified of choosing wrong. Purposeful living, however, requires a different calculation: inaction guarantees wasted capacity while imperfect action generates data, reveals aptitudes you didn't know existed, and opens doors invisible from your starting position.

Your unique calling exists because specific people need exactly what you're equipped to offer. Your continued waiting means their continued lack. Somewhere, someone needs the particular combination of pain you've survived and skills you've developed. They aren't awaiting your perfection—they're simply awaiting your beginning.

Living Out Your Purpose Through Service and Creativity

Service rewires everything. Not because it makes you morally superior, but because it fundamentally alters what you notice. When you spend Saturday morning serving meals at a shelter, your brain stops rehearsing old arguments and starts tracking need: the veteran who takes coffee but won't make eye contact, the mother who asks for two portions though she arrived alone, the teenager whose shoes are falling apart.

This attentional shift moves beyond superficial change, fundamentally altering perception. Studies confirm that consistent acts of service reduce rumination, lower stress hormones like cortisol, and activate the brain's reward centers, producing a "helper's high" that outlasts manufactured pleasures. You discover purpose not by introspection alone but by extending your hands outward. The irony of aloneness is that your healing accelerates when you stop fixating on your own wounds.

But service must be concrete, not theoretical. Signing up for abstract "volunteer opportunities" creates zero momentum. Instead, identify one specific recurring need: tutoring immigrant children every Tuesday, delivering groceries to homebound seniors Thursdays, answering crisis hotline calls twice monthly. Regularity matters because transformation happens through repetition, not inspiration. The first week feels meaningful, the third week feels routine, and by the seventh week something shifts—you're no longer doing service to fix yourself. You're serving because someone genuinely needs what only your presence provides.

God designed you for contribution, not consumption. Your skills, experiences, and even your wounds equip you to meet needs others can't perceive.

Aloneness doesn't disqualify you from this calling. It clarifies it.

Eleanor Whitman discovered her purpose in the most unlikely place: grief support groups she initially hated attending. Widowed at forty-three, she spent eighteen months barely functioning, attending sessions only because her sister insisted. But around month seven, something shifted. She noticed a pattern—newly grieving participants would arrive, stunned and silent, and within weeks start repeating the same destructive patterns she'd navigated: selling houses impulsively, dating too quickly, making financial decisions from panic rather than clarity. She started staying after sessions, offering coffee and her phone number to newcomers. No advice, just availability. Within a year, she'd become an informal mentor. Within three, she'd completed formal grief counseling certification.

She had a unique ability to translate devastation into practical next steps.

Your deepest pain, fully processed, often points directly toward your most meaningful contribution. Not because suffering is noble, but because you've developed rare insight into specific struggles. Research consistently links volunteering with positive health outcomes, particularly when the motivation is genuinely altruistic rather than self-focused. Your body knows the difference between transactional service and authentic contribution.

The persistent noticing of unaddressed problems isn't randomity's diagnostic. What breaks your heart reveals your calling.

Creative expression taps into something ancient and divine—the same force that breathed the universe into being. Writing, painting, composing music, woodworking, gardening: these aren't mere hobbies. They're sacred acts of co-creation, processing truths that language alone cannot capture while offering the world something entirely new.

Consider how Creative Aging programs transform individual pursuits into communal healing. Studies from the National Endowment for the Arts and Lifetime Arts reveal that seniors participating in visual arts or storytelling experience profound shifts—reduced loneliness, renewed purpose, deeper social connections. What begins as quiet noticing in solitude becomes a gift that serves others, turning personal expression into shared meaning.

But here's the warning: creative work fails when it becomes performative. When you create for validation rather than genuine expression, you've lost the thread. The signs are unmistakable, obsessively checking responses, abandoning projects that don't generate immediate praise, feeling worthless when work goes unnoticed.

Creativity rooted in purpose creates whether anyone's watching. It serves you first, processing grief, articulating hope, discovering hidden capacities. Only then does it extend naturally outward.

Discipline matters more than the medium. Even fifteen minutes twice weekly builds muscle. Solitude becomes your laboratory sacred space where authentic offerings take shape, uncontaminated by others' expectations, transforming your alone time into meaningful contribution.

Each morning, commit to intentional planning. Open your journal and outline one act of service alongside one creative practice for the week ahead. Assign specific time blocks to each—not vague intentions, but concrete appointments with yourself and your purpose.

Theoretical commitment crumbles without structure. Your Tuesday evening becomes your volunteer shift. Saturday morning transforms into sacred creative time—whether you're writing, painting, or gardening. These aren't suggestions; they're non-negotiable appointments with the life God designed for you.

Now, here's where magic happens: fuse your practices together. Document stories while volunteering at the shelter. Knit prayer shawls that marry craft with compassion. Teach art to seniors. Write encouragement notes to those behind bars. Compose simple songs for children's ministry. When service meets creativity, your purpose multiplies exponentially.

Build external scaffolding around your intentions. Prepay for that pottery class. Publicly commit to the library book club. Schedule recurring calendar reminders that won't let you forget. Waiting for readiness guarantees inaction.

Track your practices for thirty days, noting what energizes versus what obligates. Double down ruthlessly on what generates life; release without guilt what drains you. Purpose evolves through discovery, not theory.

Rhythm matters more than intensity. Fifteen minutes of daily creative work outperforms sporadic weekend marathons every time.

This approach transforms your solitude into generative, sacred ground where purpose flourishes.

Overcoming Barriers to Pursuing Your Purpose Alone

Begin by identifying what truly immobilizes you. Not the comfortable abstraction of "fear," but the precise words your internal critic whispers when you dare imagine more. Set aside seven uninterrupted minutes and write without censoring: "When I consider pursuing my purpose alone, the voice that stops me says..." Don't interpret or soften what emerges. Transcribe the actual catastrophe, the cruel comparisons, the meticulously constructed case against your worthiness.

These internal barriers typically fall into three distinct patterns: worthiness deceptions ("My brokenness disqualifies me from God's use"), competence deceptions ("I lack the necessary skills or credibility"), and timing deceptions ("I've already missed my opportunity"). Each requires its own spiritual dismantling. When worthiness stands as your barrier, examine the biblical figures God chose despite profound failure—not the Sunday school versions, but their actual wreckage. Moses was a murderer. David orchestrated adultery and conspiracy. Peter denied Christ at His darkest hour. God's consistent pattern isn't human perfection; it's humble availability.

Competence barriers demand honest distinction between legitimate skill gaps and perfectionism masquerading as prudence. Perhaps you genuinely need counseling training before offering guidance—then research one actionable step forward this week. But if you've been "preparing" for eighteen months while taking no tangible action, you're not being careful. You're hiding. True competence develops through imperfect practice, not endless theoretical readiness.

Timing deceptions require the most courageous confrontation.

Write your current age at the top of a blank page. Below it, catalog precisely what another year of waiting will cost you: specific opportunities lost, another season of unfulfilled calling, twelve more months your unique wound remains unhealed in others who desperately need your particular testimony. Make it concrete. Make it hurt.

Create what I call a prayer of exposure—raw, unedited confession of the fears you've kept carefully hidden even from yourself. Speak this prayer aloud daily for fourteen consecutive days, directly naming self-doubt as the liar it has always been. Simultaneously, commit to one small contradictory action each week: if competence whispers, you're unqualified, teach one person something you genuinely know. If timing insists you've waited too long, send one email today initiating what you've postponed.

Document these actions without self-judgment or performance metrics. Self-doubt doesn't surrender to willpower or positive thinking—it loses power through consistent exposure and direct contradiction. Your internal barriers diminish not when you finally feel confident, but when you choose obedience despite their relentless noise.

External barriers lack the psychological intimacy of self-doubt, yet they wield equal power to derail your calling. Society weaponizes your aloneness through relentless messaging that solo living indicates failure, that purposeful work requires institutional validation, that meaningful contribution demands applause. These pressures operate most insidiously through silence, the family members who change subjects when you mention your vision, the church culture celebrating couples' ministry while overlooking solitary service, the economic systems punishing single-income households.

You cannot eliminate these pressures.

But you can strategically construct protection against them. Build your community with surgical precision. Identify two or three individuals who demonstrate actual support through concrete actions, not theoretical encouragement. Look for those asking specific questions about your progress, offering tangible resources, celebrating small milestones without requiring your success to validate their advice. Schedule monthly accountability conversations with at least one of them. Make these appointments as non-negotiable as medical checkups, because your purpose deserves that level of commitment.

When societal pressure intensifies—relatives questioning your choices at gatherings, algorithms showing you everyone else's partnerships, moments when your solo path feels unbearably lonely—return to documented evidence of what God has already accomplished through your obedience. Reread your journal entries from six months ago. Notice the specific ways your faithful action has already created impact, however modest. This practice grounds you in accurate remembrance when cultural narratives distort your perception, reminding you that God's approval outweighs every human opinion.

The path forward requires daily practice of living your purpose despite every voice insisting you need permission you'll never receive. This unglamorous, relentless practice marks the true beginning of embodying your calling—not when circumstances align perfectly, but when you choose faithful action in the face of opposition.

Chapter 12

Your New Beginning: Committing to Your Thriving Solo Life

Reflecting on Your Journey

After a spouse dies, many widowed individuals report experiencing their first genuine moment of joy within the first two years—not constant happiness, but a single unguarded laugh or morning without suffocating grief.

Such small moments offer significant indicators of progress. Milestones in healing accumulate quietly: the Tuesday you realize you haven't checked your phone for validation in hours, the Sunday you attend church without scanning for coupled friends, the Thursday when loneliness visits but no longer dominates your entire day. These occurrences, though not spectacular, provide tangible evidence of your journey.

You have made significant progress since the initial devastation. You stopped performing grief for others, discerning which friends offered genuine support and which expected you to minimize your pain for their comfort. You discovered that 3 AM silence could shift from panic to quiet contemplation. Your kitchen table became a space for spiritual reflection, just as sacred as any formal place of worship.

Recognizing growth requires concrete accounting. What could you not do six months ago that you can do now? What terrified you in January that you handled, however imperfectly, by June? Document these shifts deliberately. This process helps you acknowledge your journey and find meaning through challenges you never wanted to cross—yet did, because God's strength carried you through.

Words on a page have power—they transform swirling thoughts into something solid, something you can hold and examine. When insights remain trapped inside your mind, they shift and blur. But articulating what you've learned during your solo season brings clarity that changes everything.

Open your journal. Write this question at the top: What have I learned about myself during this season alone?

Don't worry about making it sound beautiful or spiritual. Focus on truth. Maybe you discovered strength you never knew existed—the night you chose prayer over panic, or the morning you woke up grateful instead of grieving. Perhaps you confronted uncomfortable truths: lingering resentment toward God, or the realization that your identity was borrowed from someone else's presence. Write what's real, not what sounds impressive.

Now ask yourself: How has my relationship with God shifted? Be honest about both victories and struggles. Has Scripture become refuge rather than duty? Do you still wrestle with feeling abandoned despite believing otherwise? Document the practices that genuinely connected you to divine presence, and acknowledge the ones that felt hollow.

God values authentic conversation over polished testimony. These written insights become your roadmap forward, revealing patterns to embrace and obstacles to address with compassion and faith.

Discovering truths about yourself, God's presence in isolation, or new strengths means little without action. Knowledge alone changes nothing unless you integrate these revelations into your daily life.

Without a commitment plan, you'll drift back toward old patterns, the ones that left you feeling incomplete, perpetually waiting for external circumstances to validate your worth. Start with three concrete decisions. Not aspirations—decisions. What specific practices discovered during solitude will you protect regardless of future relationships or changing circumstances? Maybe it's your Tuesday morning prayer time, the creative work that revealed hidden capacities, or the boundary that taught you self-respect.

Write these down with embarrassing specificity: exact times, exact locations, exact frequency. Vague commitments like "stay connected to God" evaporate under pressure. "Pray in the blue chair at 6:15 a.m. before checking my phone" endures because it requires no interpretation.

Next, identify your three greatest vulnerabilities, the situations that historically unravel your hard-won stability. For many, it's romantic possibility that triggers abandonment of established rhythms. For others, it's family criticism or financial anxiety. Name what threatens to dismantle the sanctuary you've built, then create specific contingency plans. When this happens, I will do this. Not "try harder" or "be more disciplined"—actual behavioral commitments that protect what matters.

Finally, schedule your first accountability conversation within seventy-two hours. Choose someone who's witnessed your transformation and ask them this question: "What changes have you noticed in me, and what would concern you if I lost?"

The foundation of a thriving solo life is built through intentional effort, not left to chance.

Creating Your Commitment Plan

Transformation doesn't announce itself with trumpets. It shows up in the ordinary Tuesday morning when you realize you've stopped flinching at silence.

Before you commit to anything forward-facing, you need to name what's actually changed. Not what you wish had changed or what sounds impressive in a testimony—what has genuinely shifted in the bedrock of your daily existence. Can you pray now without someone else's words in your mouth? Do you make decisions based on conviction rather than consensus? When did you last check your phone out of panic versus purpose?

Write down three specific moments from the past six months that would have been impossible a year ago. Not vague spiritual feelings—concrete instances. Maybe it's the Saturday you spent eight hours alone without manufactured noise. Maybe it's declining an invitation that would have compromised your morning prayer rhythm. Maybe it's the bank account that no longer terrifies you because you finally know exactly what's in it.

Specificity matters because memory is a liar; it will convince you nothing has moved when everything has.

The growth you've cultivated builds your foundation. You've dedicated yourself to solitary work others avoid confronting deeper truths without an audience, establishing unapplaud routines, mastering unrequested skills. This deep engagement shapes your authentic life. Recognizing this fundamentally changes what you prioritize and protect going forward.

Margaret, sixty-three, sat in her kitchen eighteen months after her husband died and wrote what she wanted the next five years to look like. Not resolutions. Not bucket-list fantasies. Faith-aligned goals with her name on them.

She didn't write "be happier" or "grow closer to God"—abstractions that sound spiritual but measure nothing. She wrote: "Lead a monthly Scripture study for widows at my church by September. Save $12,000 for the Ireland pilgrimage I've delayed for thirty years. Volunteer at the hospice where James died, twice monthly, because I know that particular darkness and someone needs a guide." Each goal emerged directly from her solitude work, built on capacities her alone time had revealed.

Her goals shared three elements: they named specific actions with clear timelines, they drew on strengths her wilderness season had cultivated, and they served something beyond her comfort.

Not one goal mentioned finding another relationship or returning to who she'd been before loss.

That's what faith-aligned goals do—they acknowledge who God is shaping you to become now, not who you're trying to resurrect from before the wilderness. They transform your solitude from something you survived into the foundation for everything you build next.

Margaret's Ireland pilgrimage goal seemed straightforward on paper—$12,000 divided by sixty months equals $200 monthly. She hadn't counted on her furnace dying in February or her daughter's emergency childcare crisis requiring three unpaid days off work.

Goals need action plans that anticipate resistance.

When she broke "lead a monthly Scripture study" into sequential steps, reality emerged: approach her pastor by a specific date, recruit four committed participants before going public, prepare the first three sessions completely before launch. She scheduled every step in her calendar with buffer time, transforming aspiration into appointment. Her plan also named what would sabotage her—Sunday fatigue skipping preparation, the voice claiming she wasn't qualified, fear that nobody would show.

For each obstacle, she built a countermeasure.

Sunday prep happened Saturday mornings when energy peaked. Ruth, whose faith she trusted, reviewed her first lesson and spoke truth when imposter thoughts surfaced. She committed to hold that first session even with two people, because obedience isn't measured by attendance. Action plans fail at the same point: the week you don't feel like it.

Margaret's plan included a powerful anchor for vanishing motivation—her purpose served women needing to know they weren't alone in grief, a goal surpassing comfort.

That sentence carried her through four uncertain months.

Margaret understood something crucial: good intentions collapse without witness. She needed someone who would notice if she quit.

She asked Ruth to meet monthly for fifteen minutes—not casual coffee but structured review. Ruth received a one-page update listing Margaret's four measurable goals and the specific actions taken. This friction mattered. Research from Dominican University of California confirms that individuals sharing progress with an accountability partner achieve goals at significantly higher rates. Knowing Ruth expected numbers transformed abstract commitment into tangible output. When Margaret skipped her Ireland fund deposit twice in November, naming this aloud to someone who cared created productive discomfort that vague guilt never could. Ruth didn't shame her. She asked one question: "What adjustment makes December different?"

Accountability requires specificity and appropriate intensity.

For daily disciplines like morning prayer, Margaret used a tracking app that sent results to her spiritual director weekly—low stakes but visible. For her Scripture study leadership, she joined a quarterly peer group of small group leaders who shared attendance patterns and curriculum struggles. The framework matched the goal's weight. Daily practices need light touches; significant commitments demand human witness.

She also built environmental accountability—obstacles that made quitting harder than continuing. She prepaid six months of her creative writing workshop, losing money if she stopped attending. She posted her Scripture study dates publicly three months ahead, creating social cost to cancellation. These weren't manipulations but infrastructure, acknowledging that her future self would face discouragement her present self couldn't imagine. This leverages public commitment, which research demonstrates significantly increases adherence to stated intentions.

The most powerful accountability came from those she served. When Linda thanked Margaret for creating space where her grief finally felt normal, Margaret understood this wasn't about her anymore. Purpose creates its own gravity. People depending on what you've built sustains commitment when personal motivation evaporates entirely—and it will.

Embracing Your New Beginning

To fully appreciate your personal growth, dedicate one uninterrupted hour this week. With a physical calendar or journal, mark concrete changes across three categories: spiritual shifts, practical competencies, and relational patterns. For spiritual shifts, identify specific moments—when you first prayed without external prompts, the Scripture passage that resonated deeply beyond obligation, or the morning you recognized God's presence without needing mediation. Avoid vague statements like "my faith grew stronger." Instead, record the date you spent three hours in silence, free from panic.

Practical competencies demand equal specificity. When did you first cook a full meal instead of eating cereal for dinner? What month did you stop checking your bank balance with dread? Which skill—budgeting, changing the furnace filter, navigating conflict without apologizing for existing—would have seemed impossible eighteen months ago? Write these down with dates, because your brain will absolutely try to convince you none of it counts.

Relational patterns reveal the most.

Note the first time you said no without elaborate justification, the friendship you stopped forcing, the moment you chose solitude over mediocre company without guilt. Track when you stopped performing for approval. These shifts aren't minor adjustments—they're evidence of fundamental transformation that God has been orchestrating through your season of aloneness.

Once you've documented these shifts, create a short written statement—three to five sentences—acknowledging what this season has actually built. Read it aloud. Not to anyone else, just to yourself, standing up, with your full voice. Say the specific ways you are different now. Margaret's read: "I've learned to pray honestly instead of performing spirituality. I manage money without terror. I can sit with grief without needing someone to fix it. I know my voice matters enough to lead others."

This statement becomes your benchmark when doubt arrives—and it will. You are a different person now than when devastation first arrived.

Your commitment plan provides the infrastructure to carry you when enthusiasm wanes. This drop-off is predictable, often occurring around March when winter persists and initial goals seem pointless.

Start by writing three specific commitments for the next ninety days. Not "be more faithful" or "stay positive." Concrete actions with dates: Continue morning prayer at 6:15 AM five days weekly. Attend community group every Thursday regardless of how drained you feel. Volunteer at the food bank the second Saturday of each month. Each commitment should connect directly to the growth you've documented—the prayer rhythm you've built, the community engagement you've practiced, the service that shifts your focus outward.

Now identify what will try to stop you.

Saturday mornings you'll want to sleep in. Thursday evenings when showing up feels unbearable. The voice insisting none of this matters because you're still alone. For each obstacle, build a pre-decided response. Lay out clothes the night before. Text your community group leader by Wednesday confirming attendance. Keep the quote from the mother you helped last month visible on your bathroom mirror.

Choose one person who will receive monthly updates—not encouragement, but actual accountability. Someone who will ask the uncomfortable question when you've skipped commitments twice: "What needs to change?" This can't be someone who lets you off easy. A landmark study by the Dominican University of California revealed that individuals who wrote down their goals, shared them with an accountability partner, and sent weekly progress updates achieved 76% of their goals—a significantly higher rate than those who kept commitments private.

Finally, recognize that your plan will need adjustment. Review it monthly, not to abandon commitments when they're hard, but to distinguish between productive discomfort and genuinely unsustainable choices. This roadmap focuses on building a sustainable life, one that honors the growth God fostered during your solitude. It's designed to carry you when emotions falter, loneliness resurfaces, and self-doubt sets in.

Remember, you've already navigated greater challenges.

Conclusion

When you first opened The Art of Being Alone, you likely felt a whisper of longing or perhaps a quiet ache within your spirit. You may have found yourself navigating unfamiliar terrain, whether it was the silence following a relationship's end, the profound emptiness left by an irreplaceable loss, or simply the persistent feeling of not quite fitting in, standing on the periphery while others lived lives filled with connection. Your previous certainties may have crumbled, leaving you with an unsettling question: Is this truly what God intends for me, this solitude? The world often shouts a different narrative, equating being alone with being incomplete, making it easy to internalize that message and feel like an unfinished canvas.

However, that initial discomfort was not a sign of your brokenness but rather an indicator of sacred work waiting to begin. You have ventured far beyond merely enduring solitude; you've begun to see it as a profound opportunity, a carefully crafted space for spiritual excavation and personal renaissance. Each chapter has offered not just solace but a toolkit for transformation, turning what once felt like a desolate landscape into fertile ground for growth. You've moved from simply being alone to consciously cultivating sacred solitude, understanding the crucial distinction between isolation that diminishes and solitude that profoundly empowers.

We began this journey by peeling back layers of grief and trauma—the searing pain of divorce, the unimaginable void left by the loss of a child—acknowledging that true healing begins not with avoidance but with the courageous act of facing your darkness head-on. You bravely opened yourself to the possibility that even in your deepest sorrow, God was not absent but intimately present, working through the very fabric of your pain. Your willingness to confront those raw emotions has been the first, most pivotal step in discovering that your capacity for resilience is far greater than you ever imagined.

We dismantled the societal myth that equates aloneness with unfulfillment, revealing how cultural narratives often obscure the profound purpose of solitude. You learned to discern the crucial difference between isolating loneliness and sacred solitude, understanding the latter as God's intentional invitation for deeper connection with self and Spirit. This foundational shift allowed you to perceive your quiet moments not as absence but as fertile ground for genuine growth.

A core outcome of our exploration has been the establishment of robust spiritual practices. We cultivated consistent prayer, transforming it into an intimate, unfiltered dialogue with God. You discovered how Scripture, integrated reflectively, becomes a living guide, offering profound clarity and comfort. These contemplative methods, from journaling to breath prayer, serve as the intentional building blocks of an unshakeable inner life, anchoring you amidst life's uncertainties.

We then bravely confronted the process of healing from past wounds that may have led to your aloneness. Realizing that surrender to God's will is a dynamic, faith-driven choice allows divine grace to mend deep pain. This healing opened the door to discovering and embracing your authentic self. Solitude became a crucible where true identity, free from external pressures, is forged, allowing you to recognize your unique gifts and passions as divine instruments for a purpose-driven life.

Beyond personal and spiritual realms, we addressed the tangible elements crucial for a thriving solo existence. You gained strategies for building financial security and independence, recognizing responsible stewardship as both a practical necessity and an expression of faith. We refined the art of creating meaningful connections without compromise, establishing healthy boundaries that protect your inner peace while fostering authentic community engagement. Ultimately, we designed purposeful routines and elucidated how to remain gracefully open to future relationships from a position of secure inner peace, guiding you toward living out your unique God-given purpose vibrantly.

Now, step into the vision of your transformed future, not as a distant dream but as the inevitable outcome of the intentional seeds you've sown. Imagine waking each morning with a deep-seated calm, a sense of purpose that resonates from within, no longer dependent on external validation to define your worth. Your home, whether bustling or quiet, feels less like an empty space and more like a sanctuary you've consciously crafted—a place for reflection, creativity, and profound divine connection.

Picture yourself navigating life's complexities with unflappable grace, secure in your financial decisions, knowing you are a wise steward of God's entrusted resources. The anxieties that once overshadowed your solitary moments have receded, replaced by a quiet confidence born from diligently built habits and deep trust in divine provision. You are no longer merely surviving; you are flourishing with intention, your days rich with activities that ignite your soul and align with your deepest values.

Envision yourself engaging with the world, not from desperate yearning but from a wellspring of authentic self-awareness and strength. You connect with others, offering genuine presence while honoring the sacred boundaries that protect your peace. Your relationships are deeper, more fulfilling, built on a foundation of wholeness, not need. This is a life where creative passions are expressed without inhibition, where unique gifts are shared generously, and where your voice, once hesitant, now rings with clarity and conviction.

This future isn't a fantasy; it is the tangible reality within your grasp, constructed brick by deliberate brick with the tools and insights you've cultivated. You are not simply waiting for life to happen; you are actively, faithfully, and joyfully creating a life so vibrant and full that companionship, should it gracefully arrive, will only enhance, never complete, the magnificent masterpiece that is already you. You are building a legacy of purpose, strength, and unwavering faith, demonstrating that to be alone is not to be less but to be profoundly, authentically more.

The insights, reflections, and strategies within these pages are not meant to reside solely in your intellect; they are a blueprint for a life actively lived and intentionally built. Your most immediate and impactful step toward solidifying this transformation is to revisit the "Creating Your Commitment Plan" outlined in Chapter 12. Take out a fresh notebook or open a digital document, and begin articulating one specific, actionable goal for your thriving solo life—something you can genuinely start and implement today.

Perhaps this means committing to a dedicated 15-minute uninterrupted prayer slot each morning, creating a sacred space that becomes non-negotiable. It could involve opening a separate savings account for your emergency fund, even if your initial deposit is a modest five dollars, starting that vital habit of financial stewardship. Maybe your next action is signing up for that online course you've long considered, investing in a skill that ignites your curiosity and potential, or identifying one local volunteer opportunity that genuinely resonates with your unique God-given gifts.

Choose one, and only one, that authentically excites you and aligns with the purpose God has revealed through your journey. Then, crucially, schedule that specific action into your calendar right now, treating it as a sacred appointment with your future self. It's not about achieving an immediate grand overhaul; it's about establishing consistent, faithful action that builds momentum. The smallest, most deliberate step taken today is the very foundation upon which the strongest, most resilient future is constructed. Do not delay; begin now.

Remember, this profound journey is not about achieving some elusive state of flawless solitude, nor is it about never again experiencing a pang of loneliness. There will inevitably be days when old narratives attempt to resurface, when the quiet hums with doubt, or when the discipline of your new routines feels weighty. This is not a failure; it is simply part of the rich, complex tapestry of the human experience, a testament to your ongoing growth. Grace is your steadfast companion on this path, inviting gentle redirection and renewed effort rather than judgment.

You possess an incredible capacity for resilience, forged in the very fires of loss and re-discovery that initially brought you to these pages. Every small act of intentionality you undertake—every whispered prayer, every boundary courageously upheld, every creative spark fanned into flame—is a profound victory that rewires your spirit. You are not starting from scratch; you are standing firmly on the bedrock of experiences that have shaped you, armed with insights and practices that are now intrinsically yours.

Trust the process you've initiated, trust the divine timing that unfolds with perfect precision, and most importantly, trust the incredible strength, wisdom, and purpose God has already placed within you. You have cultivated a life rich in meaning, grounded in faith, and capable of weathering any storm. You are not waiting to be equipped; you are already equipped. You are capable; you are growing; you are becoming.

The art of being alone is ultimately not a solitary confinement but a profound and expansive canvas upon which God paints His most intricate designs for your life. It is the quiet workshop where resilience is hammered into being, where purpose finds its clearest, most resonant voice, and where the deepest, most authentic connections are first forged with the Divine. Your season of solitude is not a temporary waiting room for life to resume but the very crucible in which your most authentic, powerful self is emerging, refined and resolute.

So step forward, not with hesitation or trepidation, but with the quiet, unwavering conviction of one who profoundly understands that to be truly alone is to be fully present—present to God's unwavering love, present to your own evolving wisdom, and ultimately, present to the world in a way you never truly could be before. Embrace the quiet, for in its depths, your new beginning sings a powerful hymn of strength, grace, and an abundantly purposeful life that transcends all circumstances.

www.ingramcontent.com/pod-product-compliance
Ingram Content Group UK Ltd.
Pitfield, Milton Keynes, MK11 3LW, UK
UKHW021432280726
14060UKWH00001BA/39

9 781945 303517